BAD

WITH

MONEY

ALSO BY GABY DUNN

I Hate Everyone But You: A Novel (with Allison Raskin)

BAD
WITH
MONEY

THE IMPERFECT ART OF GETTING YOUR
FINANCIAL SH*T TOGETHER

GABY DUNN

ATRIA PAPERBACK

New York   London   Toronto   Sydney   New Delhi

ATRIA
PAPERBACK

An Imprint of Simon & Schuster, Inc.
1230 Avenue of the Americas
New York, NY 10020

First Atria Paperback edition January 2019

ATRIA PAPERBACK and colophon are trademarks of Simon & Schuster, Inc.

For information about special discounts for bulk purchases, please contact Simon & Schuster Special Sales at 1-866-506-1949 or business@simonandschuster.com.

The Simon & Schuster Speakers Bureau can bring authors to your live event. For more information, or to book an event, contact the Simon & Schuster Speakers Bureau at 1-866-248-3049 or visit our website at www.simonspeakers.com.

Interior design by Alison Cnockaert

Manufactured in the United States of America

10   9   8   7   6   5   4   3   2   1

Library of Congress Control Number: 2018028176

ISBN 978-1-5011-7633-3
ISBN 978-1-5011-7634-0 (ebook)

CONTENTS

WHAT THEY DON'T WANT YOU TO KNOW

Here's the big secret about money: No one knows anything. Despite the endless shelves of books and countless articles about money, despite the cadre of TV shows and seminars and podcasts (including my own) teaching you how to budget and cut expenses and invest and buy a home, the reality is that no one knows anything definitive about finances. Not even the experts. *Especially* not the experts. Sorry to ruin everything.

What we call "money media" is mostly made up of very confident guessers who are super good at conveying those guesses in an entertaining way. Think about the big TV showboaters like *Mad Money's* Jim Cramer or that goddess of blazers, Suze Orman. The folks who blow air horns at people who make poor money decisions. They wear funny hats and big sunglasses as they tell that you cannot afford the new car you need so you can get your kids to school. They grin as they condemn you for not starting a retirement fund when you were in kinder-garten or for not being able to predict which stocks would go down when you first invested ten years ago. (Or heaven forbid, not investing at all!) I promise that as hot as I might look in a light-up sombrero, I won't be using those tactics here.

I'm telling you in black and white right now, I am not a money guru. I do not hold the key to the magic castle, and there is not a winning lottery ticket wedged inside these pages. So why read this book? Because I just admitted that publicly. In the introduction. Because for the past several years, I've been trying to demystify personal finance so that it becomes less scary and overwhelming for all of us, including me, and I want you to join me in that pursuit. I know what it's like to start from below ground zero with this stuff, so I'll break it down without assuming you have all of this preexisting knowledge and terminology in your back pocket—and without shaming you for not knowing everything about something most of us were never taught to begin with. What I am offering is imper-fect, and it will not solve everything, but you will learn some things that might really help you. I promise not to be boring or patronizing or offensive or manipulative along the way. I can't promise I won't put on big sunglasses at some point, but this is a book so you *probably* won't see them.

Welcome to the first honest conversation about money you've ever had.

———

As I've learned through my *Bad with Money* podcast and the reactions to articles I've written on my own money foibles, my willingness to admit what I don't know is apparently rare—rarer than I thought when I started my imperfect journey of openly sharing my problems with money. It turns out that *no one* wants to talk about money. Not the rich. Not the poor. Not anyone in between. (Which, by the way, makes you a hero for picking up this book. Quick! Buy it and run somewhere private to read it!)

In the first episode of *Bad with Money*, I asked random patrons at a coffee shop two questions. First was, "What's your favorite sex position?" Everyone was game to answer that one: reverse cowgirl, missionary, 69. (I'm kidding. No one's favorite is 69.) Even the barista jumped in with an enthusiastic "doggy style!" I heard it all. Then I asked people how much money was in their bank accounts. Everyone was horrified. "That's a very personal question!" I heard amid gasps. People probably would have rather showed me their browser histories. (And to be honest, I would have liked to see them! I'm a perv!)

Clearly, money is a subject no one wants to dissect. So let's start this book by addressing the first big obstacle I faced when confronting my own money issues: stigma. Stigma, other than being a term for the sexy parts of a flower, is defined by the *Cambridge Dictionary* as "a strong feeling of disapproval that most people in a society have about something, especially when this is unfair" (you'll hear that word a lot in this book, because FINANCE IS RIGGED AF). Stigma stifles the flow of information about something so essential to our lives and it leads us to the three buzzkill Musketeers: Shame, Embarrassment, and Anxiety.

In a world where talking about money is considered taboo

or tacky, money problems are personal failings, and no one wants to hear us complain. It's no wonder that we find ourselves confused and struggling, in need of someone to blow an air horn in our faces. We have to open up about our experiences with money—the good, the bad, and especially the ugly. Otherwise there's nothing specific to learn. In fact, if you listen closely, you'll notice that so-called money experts hardly ever use exact amounts. Speaking in specifics is risky, but speaking in platitudes appeals to broader audiences.

No one likes admitting they're doing something wrong, or that they might not know what they're doing at all. I felt the same way: I thought everything was my fault, and I didn't want to be yelled at. I hate being judged as if I'm ignorant for not knowing something "obvious." I would do anything to avoid that judgment. I'd denounce Janelle Monáe. Climb the Andes naked. Brush my teeth with salt rocks.

I want to be able to talk about the ways the system is stacked against us, without worrying about being labeled "lazy." My research has led me to conclude that (1) the system is definitely stacked against us (unless you're a millionaire who picked up this book to mock *me* personally) but that (2) there are positive steps we can take to make our money lives easier within that very flawed system.

The prevailing narrative goes that if you're bad with money, you're naive and irresponsible or defective in some other big way. Because of that, you should keep that information to yourself, and if anyone finds out that you're bad with money, you should be ashamed. MOREOVER: If you're not actively trying to change your situation with intense strategies like strict budgets and financial fad diets that no person can possibly maintain forever, then you're a bad person who deserves the bad situation you've found yourself in. The only thing people love more than having money is judging other people for how they're using their money. (Example: "My money situation isn't great but at least I'm not like my irresponsible cousin Terry! Why do you have an Equinox membership if you never go to the gym, Terry?!")

This narrative is an extension of the prosperity gospel, which posits that if you are truly a good, smart, and worthy person, you will magically prosper. Even people who know this isn't true have largely internalized the message. Hell, this is what I thought about myself until recently. I'm a confident person, successful in my career, happy in my love life, surrounded by friends, close to my sister, and I still believed that because I didn't have a handle on my money situation, I must be a bad human and a worthless failure. How could I know any differently? My friends who had jobs didn't discuss their salaries, and my friends without jobs never explained where their money came from or revealed that they were struggling. I figured everyone around me knew something I didn't.

It came to a head for me after college. I spent my early 20s working as a freelance writer/reporter, with the occasional 9-to-5 reporting gig at various publications. When I was freelancing, I always felt deeply mortified to press the magazines or blogs I was writing for to give me my owed paychecks—which were *always* late (#freelancelyfe). If you've ever been a freelancer, you are aware of the cruel truth that a place that owes you money is never in ANY hurry to send you your check. Big payment, small payment: It doesn't matter. Trying to get paid becomes its own full-time job. I worried that if I needed money (as a 20-something living in New York City, no duh, of course I did), I would look desperate. The optics of seeming like a "carefree New York hipster debutante" to some strangers in *Cosmo* magazine's accounts payable department was more important to me than actually having money in my checking account.

Sometimes I had to literally beg in multiple emails for freelance jobs to pay me specifically because rent was due and I had nothing. (And I would tell them that! Horrifying!) Once it took a whole year for a major international publication to cut me a $500 check. And instead of being angry at them, I was MORTIFIED that I needed that money so badly. It made me feel pathetic and unimportant. They should have been embarrassed by their shitty treatment of a freelancer, but they weren't. I was.

Don't get me wrong: I was delighted by the bylines I got in *Playboy* and the *New York Times Magazine*. I posted about them on Facebook and received all the comments and likes and validation I could have ever wanted. People thought I was thriving. They thought I was successful. Maybe they thought I was making good money.

The negative side of my freelancing life never made it to my Facebook feed. I did not have the chance to connect to anyone else struggling financially because I never revealed that *I* was struggling financially. But if everyone was pretending, then how could anyone figure out anything useful?

During college in Boston, two of my friends and I lived cheaply in a shitty house where we saved money in a jar labeled "Beer, Bread and Bitches." We had no decorations in our apartment, and anyone who needed a place to crash could sleep on the living room floor. We ate mostly homemade pasta with butter. We wore clothes from the Garment District, a warehouse thrift shop in Cambridge with no regard for sturdiness or cleanliness. (Maybe too little regard. My ex-boyfriend got scabies from going through its $1 bargain bin.)

When I graduated from college and moved to New York, I lived rent free on my brother's couch, an hour outside the city, while I looked for a job. I finally found one, writing about movies for AOL, and immediately moved in with a stranger in a Chinatown apartment where my room did not have a full wall to separate it from hers. It was not a very livable apartment. (For example, the floors were uneven, which I found out when I tried to scramble eggs for the first time.) The people I hung out with in NYC, no matter their race or age, all had vague jobs: Musicians? Students? Writers? Ironic tattoo aficionados? I had no idea. Just like in Boston, everyone behaved as if they were on the same financial playing field without ever discussing it with anyone else.

I started getting into light credit card debt. I moved a lot because I couldn't afford anything long term. I always figured that one day, I'd get paid some sort of huge lump sum that would all at once solve my financial problems.

Living day-to-day came naturally to me. My whole life, my dad was thousands of dollars in debt from alcoholism, addiction, and gambling. On my podcast, he admitted to being "reckless and selfish" and to encouraging my mom to live in the moment too. They spent money on vacations, clothes, parties, and furniture our family could not afford. There was no thinking about the future. "Look," he argued in his own defense, "it may have not been a good lesson, but we had a great time."

This dynamic continues. Whereas in some families, a child in her 20s might call to ask her parents for career or money advice, my dad has called to ask *me* for help with salary negotiation. In the first episode of my podcast, my dad actually revealed that the very day we recorded, he'd been let go from his job working in addiction recovery therapy. When I asked if he was okay, he casually and optimistically said, "I'll probably get something I'd rather be doing anyway." He often tells me "the universe will provide." But in all my years of life thus far, the universe has yet to sign any of my checks.

1

YOUR ROOTS ARE SHOWING

I grew up in a one-story red-roof house in Hollywood, Florida, with my mom, my dad, my older brother, and my younger sister. Our house was on Fillmore Street, in a line of streets named for the US presidents. (That explains why I know something about our thirteenth president, Millard Fillmore, last of the Whig party.)

It was a warm house and very lived in—lots of sports memorabilia on the walls and records lying around and a fish tank and trunks full of dress-up old clothing. The floors were yellow tile, with occasional little leaf designs painted on here and there.

The backyard had a banana tree, an avocado tree, and a grapefruit tree. I could climb to my heart's content, and we could practically live off the land. (I thought every salad had all three ingredients until high school.) My dad had dug up the front yard and put in sand and mulch. He planted cacti and Joshua trees and "tumbleweeds" to make it look like a Wild West scene. It was the only house on the block without a normal yard, and sometimes I'd catch people driving by just to marvel at it. When I didn't know about other people's houses, I thought ours was the best one in the world.

When I was 15, my dad was struggling to figure out his job situation, and we had to move. My brother, 30 then, had gone to New York City. My grandmother, who'd lived with us for a while, had passed away after a terrible battle with cancer. It was just me, my sister, my dad, and my mom with both an extra bedroom and a big, beautiful backyard we didn't "need."

My dad tells me they bought that house in 1987 for $170,000. (By comparison, the houses I look at now on Zillow on Los Angeles' East Side are often $1 million or more. Oh, the '80s. You were prosperous.) We then sold the Fillmore Street house for $350,000 in 2002. At the time, my parents also took my younger sister out of an expensive private school—which we couldn't afford—to enroll her in Pioneer Middle, a local public school. For my sister to qualify to attend that school, we had to live in that district. They wanted her to go to Pioneer so she could transition into the A-rated public school, Cooper City High (again avoiding private school tuition). The public high school near our old house in Hollywood had a reputation for stabbings, so they wanted her in a free, and better, environment. (It's slim pickings anyway: Florida ranks twenty-ninth in the United States in quality of high school education.) The house we moved to in Cooper was smaller and cost $275,000.

The sale of the house should have been a coup for us

Dunns. But even more immediate than our family's money troubles were my dad's excessive drinking and drugging. He couldn't keep jobs. He was gambling. It all went hand in hand. (He's not shy about his past. He'll be the first to tell you stories of his pre-sobriety days if you ask him. Actually, don't ask him. You'll never shut him up.)

———

On a recent Thanksgiving trip home, I rediscovered my early-teen-years diary and was surprised to see that I wrote about money *a lot*. In September 2002, I wrote that I had complained about my eyesight and my dad told me he didn't want to "waste money" on an eye doctor visit. (I'm not sure if we had health insurance at the time.) I recounted how he and I went to the local pharmacy and picked up cheap eyeglasses that weren't my prescription. When those didn't work, he gave me my little sister's old eyeglasses, again not my prescription. In my entry about this, I despaired about the glasses being ugly, too small for my face, and not the right lenses. I decided not to wear glasses at all. (I currently wear glasses, so I guess there really was something wrong with my eyes.)

I also mentioned a few times in the diary how worried I was about my mom's spending at expensive stores like Bebe and Gucci, most often on gifts for my little sister, who to this day continues to enjoy the finer things.

In January 2003, I wrote in my journal, "On the way home, my mom asked why I had yelled at my sister in Aber- crombie. I told her that either she should stop complaining about how broke we are or stop buying my sister clothes she doesn't need." Once home, I chronicled how my mom and dad got into a fight about money: "My mom screams at my dad to work harder cuz we have no money. Gee wiz, I wonder the fuck why?"

I remember that as a teenager, I had been aware of our money problems, but I didn't realize until I reread this diary just how much financial anxiety I had or how much we were struggling at certain points. (We were mostly decidedly middle class.) I felt responsible for convincing my parents to see the error of their ways. I felt resentment for my sister's insistence on buying new stuff all the time, and for my mom's reluctance to tell her no. I felt helpless to change the situation because I was only a kid. But my parents are not bad people. Not only is their way of life super common, my dad was also contending with a disease and my mom with the consequences of that disease. They really did the best that they could with the hand we were dealt.

———

By now, both of my parents are very tired of being interrogated about their finances by their older daughter. (My dad finished his interview for the podcast in 2016 with, "Did you get what you wanted?") My money questions have hit a collective family nerve, but I was determined to get to the bottom of what they taught me about money—lessons delivered both consciously and subconsciously.

A financial psychologist I spoke to on my podcast, Dr. Brad Klontz, says that people's families create different money scripts—the messages we have internalized about money, like "money can solve all your problems and bring you happiness," or "you need to treat yourself when you're feeling sad," can be categorized broadly as "wealthy" or "poor." The terms *wealthy* and *poor* here have more to do with the quality of your view of money than how much money you actually have. An example of a wealthy money script would be prudently saving money in case of an emergency, and a poor money script would be the assumption that money is bad and that wealthy people are inherently evil. Parents and older family members, the first role models we really encounter, have a huge impact on our financial views. We watch the way they interact with money, and what we see shapes how we go on to spend and save. As with anything else that we absorb early on, unlearning this stuff is a serious undertaking.

———

I can't analyze the money scripts my dad passed on to me without first looking at the ones he inherited from my grandmother, Meme. She's a Holocaust survivor, and the effects of her time in concentration camps have reverberated throughout our family. I've felt it in the whispers among my dad and his sister and my mom about "what happened to her."

When I was a little kid, I didn't appreciate Meme. She didn't dress like the other grandmothers—my sister's friends nicknamed her "Juicy" because she was as flashy and trendy as a pair of rhinestone Juicy sweatpants. She never acted like the other grandmothers either: she often ditched us for hair appointments or nice dinners with friends. I thought she was kind of mean. As I got older, I stopped taking her personality personally. Now I love goading her into giving me her harsh opinions on everything. She often calls me "a very interesting girl." It's not said with derision, but it's not said with pride either.

All my life, I've heard that Meme and her husband, Pepe, had a lot of money that they were withholding from the rest of the family. The implication was that we kids had to go through Meme to get to Pepe's money. She helped pay for bat mitzvah dresses and summers at sleepaway camp. But she also has strong views on when to lend (and when not to) that seem to lack a sense of empathy or selflessness. (I never got to ask Pepe about his finances before he died, but if I had, I don't think he would have been open to talking about them. It was probably something he'd view as uncouth.)

If Meme was boujee, then my mom's mom, Lee, was our working-class hero. A frequent source of sadness for me growing up was Lee's inability to move down to Florida from my mom's native New York to be close to us because she couldn't afford to quit her job. When I was a kid, I wrote a letter to her boss in crayon begging him to let her retire, a word I knew only because she and my mom talked about it endlessly. "It's not that Grandma doesn't love you," my mom would say. "She just can't retire yet."

I adored Lee. I hated how neither she nor my parents could fund her move. Once she finally did retire and come to Florida, she almost immediately was diagnosed with colon cancer and died at only 68. This fueled my theory that your days are numbered and even if you did the right thing and retired only when it was responsible to do so, you could still up and die without ever enjoying your freedom.

I'm sure Meme feels the same way, and I can't blame her. Once she was liberated from the concentration camps, she married an American soldier and emigrated from Paris to South Bend, Indiana, of all places. She gave birth to my father when she was 20 years old, had another daughter, and went through one more husband, an abusive man, before meeting my grandfather Pepe in the 1950s. Pepe was an anesthesiologist who made good money and was well regarded in the community. Meme and Pepe absolutely loved each other, but as Marilyn Monroe said in the film *Gentlemen Prefer Blondes*, "Don't you know that a man being rich is like a girl being pretty? You wouldn't marry a girl just because she's pretty but my goodness, doesn't it help?"

After they were married, Meme bought expensive jewelry, antique art, and fine clothing. Pepe wore cashmere sweaters and nice watches. (When he passed away, I inherited a Burberry scarf.)

"So you guys were rich?" I asked.

"We were comfortable. I don't call it rich." (Classic Meme dodge.)

———

Asking your family specific money questions is like opening Pandora's box. I have one friend who spends all of April silencing her dad's phone calls because it stresses her out too much to hear about their taxes. Most of my peers don't know the full extent of their family's money histories. If you don't ask the questions, you never have to think about it, and most of my friends don't want to think about it. If I didn't know the reality of my family's financial situation, I could pretend it wasn't so fraught. If I hadn't sat down to interview my family members, I wouldn't have to face this truth: how Meme and Pepe saved and spent while my parents struggled. It's a hard pill to swallow.

When I gently brought this up to her, Meme didn't apologize. I reminded her that the only time she ever directly gave me money was once when I called her crying. (A story we'll get to in Chapter 4 on unpaid internships.) As far as she can remember, she said, aside from that one time, I never *asked* her for money. She feels no remorse in not giving me what I didn't ask for. I said I normally felt too guilty to ask. I was just a kid; she was an adult. She shrugged: and said, "Tough shit." Conversation over.

If Meme was into luxury, her son, my dad, swung completely the other way. He became a flower child. Woodstock, long hair, bell-bottoms, VW vans, acid tabs. He realized the importance of money after Meme's second divorce, when he had to babysit his sister a lot more. The two kids always shared a room. Sometimes all three of them shared a studio.

My dad's first wife was a fellow hippie. They opened a handmade leather goods shop together in Gainesville, Florida, which they called MASANDU, in 1972. (Google Maps informs me that the original location is now, sadly, a Papa John's.) In 1973, my half-brother was born. My dad was gambling and drinking to excess, and his wife, who owned half of the store, wanted a divorce. Not wanting to "work for her," my dad said he cleared out the entire inventory and sold the store before she could have it, thereby winning the Petty Olympics of 1975.

In the early 1980s, he met my mom, an ambitious redhead studying law. They married in 1983. In 1988, I was born! (Hello, me! You have no idea what you're in for!)

Throughout the next decade, my dad ran a couple of businesses, but he was held back by his addictions—alcohol, gambling, and cocaine. "I had probably taken a cut in pay 'cause of my escapades," he said.

My dad was a fun, well-intentioned guy, but considering consequences and planning ahead were not really his thing. Social anxiety and insecurity led to his go-to: buying drinks for everyone in the place. Put it on your tab, and you become the most popular person in the bar.

———

My mom was more responsible, but her upbringing had also been less than stable. Her father, Harvey, was an alcoholic too, and her parents split up when she was young. Her dad fixed vending machines, sold insurance, and worked for the telephone company. At the telephone company, he stole phones and sold them on the side, which got him fired. He then drove a cab in Manhattan and fell way into debt. Harvey took out so many loans that my mom eventually had to tell the bank not to issue him any more. She suspected her father was in over his head with gambling.

My mom guessed that if my grandmother been born some decades later, she would have been a successful businesswoman. But in the 1950s, Lee's independence made her stick out in a negative way. (Harvey was interested in history, which working-class people didn't go to school for because it was seen as a waste of money.) Their low stations in life limited both of them. Their families didn't invest in their futures. Lending always came with emotional strings and judgments attached. This is why, my mom contends, she spent so much money on me and my sister.

When she was growing up, my mom worked in a drugstore in Manhattan selling makeup. After graduating from Brooklyn College, she went to law school in Florida at Nova Southeastern University while she also worked three jobs and was on food stamps. Her furniture was comprised of bricks with wooden slats. She graduated in 1980, began working in criminal law, and started paying the loans back the next year. It took her twelve years to pay them off, but she did it.

My memories of my mom in the 1990s are of her on "roller skates." It's something I used to say when I was a kid: "My mom wears roller skates to work," meaning she was always moving. I'd go to work with her, and she'd rush from one courtroom to another or from one end of her office to another. She never sat down. She wore this terrible black and yellow blazer that I called "the bumblebee" because she just looked like a blur—a flying, buzzing bee skipping from one flower to the next. She worked a lot, and even though she was always working, we never seemed to have any money to show for it.

For my whole life, my mom has been the breadwinner of our family. She still works as a divorce and child custody attorney, but recently she wasn't making enough at her private practice to continue using it as her only revenue stream, so in her 60s, she has gotten a second job reviewing legal documents. My dad is 71. He currently drives for a ride-sharing app.

We internalize our experiences and scripts at a very young age and it's really hard to make them unstick. They get passed down from generation to generation. Meme believed life was pain, so why not spend to surround yourself with beauty? And despite my dad's rebellious, hippie instincts, his disease pushed him to follow that line of thought. I watched my mom's mom, Lee, work herself literally to death, and I took away the message that it's not worth it to never spend money waiting for a day when you can. That day might never come.

In order to start deconstructing and fixing your own ways of thinking about money, you need to dig into the past and see what you were taught—consciously and subconsciously. Those messages may be burrowed deep, and at one point they may have protected you, but ask yourself: Are they still serving your best interests? Or is it time to let your family's money scripts go and make your own?

Growing up, it doesn't usually occur to you that different families have different financial situations until you start seeing the way other people live—either by sleeping over at friends' houses or observing the lifestyles of the characters on your favorite television shows. (Dial it back, *The OC*.) But still, you tell yourself you're not less than, just *different*, or that TV mansions aren't real anyway.

Despite, or maybe because of, how limited things were, I had a pretty good childhood. We always had dress-up clothes donated by my grandmas and aunt. We had Barbie dolls I destroyed with Sharpies to the face. (Sorry!) We went to McDonald's and Pizza Hut. I played outside, biking and climbing trees. I read Babysitter's Club and Nancy Drew books from both the local and school libraries. We went to free events like carnivals and parades and concerts.

I took gymnastics classes. Even though I sort of realized I couldn't buy the nicer leotards the other girls had, I still got to go to class. We went camping. We rode horses. We drove around the Smoky Mountains, went fishing, and visited Dollywood's best problematic attraction, the Dixie Stampede. And for the most part, everyone around us was on the same playing field.

When I was in second grade, my dad's alcoholism launched my mom into a journey for deeper meaning. She started attending synagogue regularly, found her own friends, and, most important, found her higher purpose. She became increasingly observant. I remember her inviting the rabbi and his wife over to help us turn our entire kitchen kosher. This meant replacing all the dishes and silverware and purchasing two different sets, which we ended up using for years—one white for dairy and one black for meat. It was an expensive and arduous undertaking.

All the other people at the synagogue sent their children to strict Jewish schools, so she switched me out of public school. We'd be paying tuition now. We started associating with different kinds of people.

At my public school, my best friend had been a girl named Madeline who lived in a small duplex with her family. Her parents were Tai Kwon Do instructors. One year for Halloween, she dressed up as a car crash victim, meaning her parents wrapped her in gauze, toilet paper, and red paint. They weren't wealthy either.

At my new all-Jewish school, the majority of the students were upper middle to upper class. That was the first time I realized I was in a somewhat lower economic bracket. For one thing, when I started there, my family still lived in the town of Hollywood, which was very un-PCly nicknamed "Hollyhood." My new school, however, had been built alongside a nicer neighborhood's Jewish Community Center so we could use its new sports facilities and big playgrounds. The school was surrounded by a thick black fence, and security guards stood at all the entrances.

Because of school uniforms, I skated by without fully realizing I was poorer than my new friends until middle school. When bar and bat mitzvah season descended, the ruse got cracked wide open. Every weekend, another kid in my grade had a huge party celebrating the transition into "adulthood." Sometimes there were even multiple parties a weekend. (More on that insanity in Chapter 12 on weddings.)

Suddenly I started becoming aware of my parents' spending, and like a rookie financial detective, tried to piece together how we were affording our new lives. Where had the money for my—and now my sister's—uniforms, books, and tuition been coming from? Where was the money for my upcoming bat mitzvah coming from? If we didn't have enough money, how had we been paying for everything before? Turns out we weren't. A lot of the money came from loans or credit cards, much of which my parents still won't reveal to me. The rest of our life was often bankrolled by my mother's bartering. Instead of taking money from clients who a lot of the time couldn't afford to pay her for her legal services, I found out my mom was rendering them for trades.

Some things we got for "free" were:

Haircuts
Nail salon visits
Flowers
Bedroom furniture
Jewelry
Party planning for my bat mitzvah
Tailors

And who knows what else? If a crate of salad dressing showed up at the house, it was probably because my mom had handled the divorce of the HR department head for Kraft. When I confronted her in fall 2016 about not really ever making the money back on the work she'd done, she replied simply, "There were children who needed my help." But she didn't have an answer when I pointed out that she too had her own children, who could have benefited from her getting paid properly.

What came next is probably familiar to any Jewish child out there: guilt. She immediately started in with: "So I guess you're saying you had a terrible childhood?" No! The opposite. My parents overspent because they wanted to give us "life experiences." The huge financial consequences of a family vacation or party, in their minds, were worth the smiles on our faces and the full photo albums. Would I trade in the time I met Cinderella at Disney World when I was 4 or attending my cousin's bat mitzvah in Israel when I was 10? The problem is that I had a great childhood. It was just one we couldn't afford.

My sister Cheyanne is three years younger than me. On an episode of my podcast, she told me that while I was hyper-aware of our family's money problems, she simply didn't realize we had them. If my sister asked my parents for money and they gave it to her, then how bad could things *really* be? I must just be paranoid. It wasn't until she was in college that my parents first told her they couldn't afford to give her money anymore.

To her credit, she went out and got a job at a restaurant— and she's had several since. (My favorite was a train-themed grill, the Midtown Caboose, in Tallahassee, Florida.) A couple years ago, having moved to LA to be near me, she had two jobs: one as a hostess and one as a personal assistant. She now works in marketing for a porn company.

There are a few luxuries she insists on. Living alone is one. Weed is the other. When I asked her if instead she might want to put that money into savings, she laughed. "Sure, yeah. Maybe. But come on. It's legal here." Would you deny a working woman the equivalent of a glass of cabernet at the end of the night? Lay off her about the weed.

I'm envious of her commitment to comfort. The reason I brought her on the podcast was to confront her. A few months before we recorded the episode, I'd loaned Cheyanne a good chunk of money to pay her bills: $1,000. It was an emergency, she said. She had called me crying. She wasn't going to be able to make rent, even with my parents' help, and also pay her gas, water, and electric bills. I had some extra income that month, and she both thanked me and apologized to me in a flip-flop of desperation. A few hours after I transferred her the money, she posted a photo of her latest purchase: $40 worth of sushi.

"I wanted to treat myself," she said when I brought it up, completely calm and not at all defensive. I informed her that you can't treat yourself with someone else's money.

"I've been so sad about money, so I need to spend money to feel better," she said. "I work five nights a week in a restaurant, so tell me I don't deserve $40 worth of sushi." (She's picked up a lot from Meme.) She paid her bills with my loan, but she also unabashedly set aside a little something-something for herself, and she wasn't afraid to show it off on social media—where anyone, including her benefactor, might see it.

She then turned the tables: Maybe it's *my* fault I feel money shame because I insisted on doing everything alone. (Damn. She's good.)

Even with the same parents, it's clear my younger sister and I were raised to have very different money scripts. I don't want to throw all the shade on my sister. My parents certainly spent money on me too.

In a 2016 interview with my mom, I wondered out loud what would have changed about our money scripts if she and my dad had told us the truth about our family's finances from the beginning. "Maybe I'm giving myself too much credit even though I was young and an asshole," I said. But what if my mom had straight up said to us, "We cannot afford this." What if they'd said no to my sister's desire for new dresses or to my entitlement to sleepaway summer camps?

"I never would have done that," my mom replied, aghast. She countered, asking me why I didn't ask more questions at the time if I was so concerned. I said when I did, I was written off as "precocious" and like Cheyanne said, "paranoid." (Being labeled "trying to be grown-up" by their families for expressing concern about money is an experience a few other young people interviewed for this book said they shared. We're seen as "little adults" when our parents want our help and as "nosy kids" when they don't.)

My sister and I lived in financial whiplash: sometimes our parents said yes to everything; sometimes they said no to things that made no sense. Our family's money reality was a mystery to us and seemed to operate primarily on whims. We each took different money scripts from that, and it wasn't until we sat down to discuss them with each other that we even got a peek at the full picture.

If you have siblings or cousins or anyone else around your age who grew up with you (or, hell, even friends who had similar households), talk to them about what they witnessed. Your money script is a puzzle, and other people hold most of the pieces. We don't always remember events from our childhoods correctly, and there is a lot we forget entirely. But it all informs our financial patterns as adults. You can only start undoing once you've finished unpacking.

TAKEAWAYS

- Everyone is affected by how their parents or guardians treat money (including your parents, their parents, their parents' parents, in one long line going back to that time God told Adam he needed to work in the Garden of Eden for his keep, but then Adam got evicted and had to figure his shit out on his own).
- Sometimes this means echoing patterns, and sometimes it means rebelling against them—for better or for worse.
- Figuring out what messages you received and why can help you decide if you like or agree with those messages, and/or what you can do to change them.

2

MY WONDER YEARS

I hated going to a private Jewish high school. I felt stifled by the forced religious aspect of my secular education. Our first "class" every morning was a prayer session, which I thought was a waste of time since God wasn't real. (Edgy.)

We also had to carve out a significant portion of our day for Torah and Talmud studies. I wasn't sure what purpose these classes served in the real world. (For this and more groundbreaking teen cynicism, don't touch that dial!)

Many of the students there were well off, which I viewed at the time as some kind of moral failing. I didn't *want* to be rich. Poverty was a virtue. I was a devotee of *RENT*, a musical about a group of delinquent artists who refuse to pay rent to their former friend and landlord, who (while doing his job) is painted as a total villain. I saw myself as one of the pure-of-heart rebels and everyone who dealt in money as sellouts.

I attended that high school on a half-tuition academic scholarship that I'd secured in eighth grade by writing an essay and passing a couple of in-person interviews. I'd attended for elementary and middle school, but high school tuition was higher. (My mom says on average it cost $7,000 to $8,000 a year for me to attend the lower grades, and then tuition doubled to $15,000 a year in high school, without the scholarship.) Many students suddenly couldn't afford to attend anymore and switched to public schools.

The students that stayed at my high school had all the usual wealth signifiers of the early aughts: aviator sunglasses, Dooney & Bourke purses, Tiffany bracelets. It was fashionable to straighten your hair until it was stick-straight, and the girls had expensive hair straighteners that made this possible. Sometimes my mom ironed my hair for me with an iron while I lay on an ironing board.

The secret breakdown of class was obvious to anyone reading the markers on the students. There was also a clear hierarchy demarcating who was able to afford tutors and who couldn't; who could afford to stay after school and participate in activities for their college applications and who couldn't. My artsy friends in different grades, many of whom were immigrants or lower middle class, had after-school jobs. Many of them came from single-parent households and were required to take on extra obligations, like driving their siblings home and watching them, that prevented them from reaching the top of the crop. It's hard to play on two sports teams and edit the yearbook when you've got three little brothers to look after.

I remember one girl at my school, an immigrant from Europe whom I had a crush on. She was a year above me, and when it came time for everyone to decide where they were going to college, she was one of the only people in her grade who simply wasn't going. I was shocked at the idea that anyone just *wouldn't go* to college. It was 2004. Every TV show on the WB had a college acceptance episode. Every movie was about finally graduating and going off to college. College was sports and romance and freedom and the future. I was confused because she was immensely talented and would have been a competitive candidate.

She told me she couldn't go to college because she was undocumented. I hadn't known that. And even if she hadn't been, her family couldn't afford it because her mother worked under the table for cash. They were personas non grata. She wasn't sure what she was going to do after graduation. Maybe stay in South Florida, live at home, and get a job. Maybe just move to a city and find a retail or service industry gig to survive.

I was so angry for her. I thought it wasn't fair that someone with direction and who worked hard, like her, wouldn't go to college. The college admissions process, it turns out, wasn't about justice. Education was directly tied to money.

When I was in high school, I worked for a time as a catering waiter at my synagogue. The temple had an in-house catering service for weddings and bar and bat mitzvahs hosted in its ballroom, and a few of the local kids worked there. We had to show up way before the event, in our black and white uniforms, and set up the whole party, which sucked. But we also got free dinners every time, which was awesome. During the cocktail hour, my job was to walk around with a tray and offer people appetizers like mushroom tarts and salmon rolls. Sometimes I manned the fruit and vegetable bar.

Every weekend we worked from 6:00 p.m. to early in the a.m. when we had to clean up the whole affair. Sometimes that required mopping up vomit from the bathroom. Sometimes it was just breaking down tables and cleaning up garbage from the dance floor (including drunk Uncle Fred!). I was paid in cash. I don't remember what my salary was, just that it was enough for me to cover whatever expenses I had as a high schooler. (Spiked chokers and black eyeliner?) I didn't save anything from that job.

I worked there for a year and was eventually let go because I kept eating the food. I would give out an appetizer and then sneak one into my mouth. Eventually someone from a wedding party noticed me doing this and rightfully complained. I was not a good catering waiter.

I was, however, a good writer. When I was 16, I got into a paid internship program at the local newspaper. I was so happy because (1) I needed a job and (2) it was actually in the field I hoped to go into. How many teenagers can say that? The program was called Next Gen, and it became one of the most consistent and treasured aspects of my high school experience. We got to attend editorial meetings at the newspaper offices, pitch our own stories, and write little articles that actually appeared in the paper with our bylines. I wrote about all sorts of topics: music reviews, profiles of Christian rock bands, ROTC champions and robotics clubs, and tips on how to decorate your locker.

When I was a senior in high school, I graduated to a job

at the neighborhood division of the paper based out of a city called Tamarac. I was officially a freelance reporter there, no longer merely a teen intern. I'd go in, get assignments, write them either before school (so at 6:00 a.m.) or after school and then they'd run in the newspaper. I was paid by the source, so for every person I interviewed, I got more money. This led to 500-word stories with seven sources. I wanted to get PAID.

Because I was still in school, I sometimes worked during class too. I often omitted my age when interviewing people. Sources, not knowing I was a high school student, would call me on my cell phone during the day for interviews. One time in AP Government class, I got a call from a source and literally looked at my teacher and said, "I have to step out and take this. It's for work." He took my phone away.

I occasionally babysat too. This was good for extra cash and I enjoyed hanging out with the kids. I met these families through my synagogue, and I'm still friends with some of my former charges on Facebook. (Yes, I am that old.)

Working with the youths is an easy-to-acquire but hard-to-do job for someone in high school. At one point, I was hired as a summer camp counselor, which required me to spend the summer in the woods in Georgia helping 13-year-old girls learn about tampons. That took care of food and lodging, but it was also a nonstop twenty-four-hour exhausting high-stakes gig.

One weird summer, I also worked as a secretary for my mom's divorce and child custody law firm, answering phones and filing paperwork. This led to many diary entries about how depressing the job was and how sad it was to see kids being used as props by their parents. I railed a lot about the injustices I was witnessing, which in the end opened my eyes to problems within our legal system—but also, at 15, it was a bit much for my brain to handle every day. (My mom is a strong woman.)

———

Jobs-wise, you kind of have to take what you can get in high school. I acquired a lot of these jobs through people I knew who took a chance on me. And if you're in high school, you're often trying to get your first job, so you don't have a full résumé to prove you're a good employee (which, obviously, does not include eating the food you're supposed to be serving on the job. Shame on you, rapscallion Gaby).

Aside from being an early way to start saving for the future, contribute to your family, or have your own spending money, getting a job in high school looks pretty good on a college application—as long as it doesn't have a negative impact on your GPA. College admissions counselors I spoke to said admissions offices take into account job experience as much as "extracurriculars" because they know that not all students can afford to not work. Don't shy away from putting your job experience on your college application too. It all counts.

If you're a high schooler (or know one) who wants or needs a job, here are some tips from my experiences:

1. **ASK EVERYONE.** Be vocal about your pursuit of a job. Ask your parents. Ask your friends' parents. Ask your teachers. If you shop at one store or eat at one restaurant a lot, ask the people working

there if they're hiring. Ask at your church or synagogue or mosque. Ask the people handing out free samples of frozen yogurt. It doesn't hurt to ask. They're only going to say yes or no, and the earth will most likely continue to orbit the sun.

2. **EMBRACE "NEPOTISM."** Many of the high schoolers I talked to told me they got their first jobs from friends who'd been promoted enough to recommend them. If you have friends who work at a certain restaurant, they can put in a good word for you (even if this will be your first job). If you have friends who have been camp counselors before, ask if they will recommend you for the summer. If you are able to score a job through your friend, remember to give it your all, because if you disappoint, it makes your friend look bad too, and you don't want to be *that* person.

3. **A JOB IS A JOB IS A JOB.** A job can mean working at a store at the mall or at an ice cream parlor, but it can also mean mowing lawns and babysitting and organizing your aunt's home office for her. These types of "neighborhood" jobs are especially useful for teenagers who are too young to be hired for certain professional opportunities.

4. **WORK THE INTERNET.** Obviously you should run everything you find by a parent or trusted adult, but consult sites like Craigslist, LinkedIn, and

HireTeen.com, all of which list job opportunities. Take advantage of your Internet savvy to find remote options. Sometimes people will post on social media about needing to hire someone to do online work for them: to run an Instagram account, write up marketing emails, or do other tasks that can be done on a computer from anywhere. These gigs can also provide flexible hours, which you'll need as a high school student with homework and exams on your plate.

5. **PUT YOUR BEST FOOT FORWARD.** Start by creating a résumé that you feel good about. There might not be a lot to put on it at first, but you can list teachers or coaches or religious leaders as references. When detailing your experience, you can put responsibilities you've had at school or your extracurricular activities—anything to show leadership and work ethic. All of it is relevant. Your résumé shouldn't be long, anyway—one page or less.

When you fill out a job application (which you can request from the manager/supervisor or find online), you should show it to someone else prior to handing it in—even a friend. Another pair of eyes might point out missing words or misspellings or some skill that you forgot to mention. Run everything you're doing by a trusted adult so that person can see if the job is safe and/or if you're presenting yourself well on paper and in interviews. (You can also google résumé help websites like ResumeRobin.com and others for tips.) Hand in the application and résumé to the *manager*, not another employee. And don't send a parent to hand in your application for you.

6. **KEEP TRYING.** Throw spaghetti at the wall and see what sticks. Apply to locations that you might think are too far away (don't just pick the Gap by your house when there are multiple locations). Be open-minded. When I was a teen, I thought it would make me cool to work at Bath and Body Works, but I wasn't getting hired there. Where you do end up doesn't say anything about your self-worth. None of my jobs allowed me to smell like Cucumber Melon mist spray, but they were all jobs just the same.

TAKEAWAYS

- High school jobs may not be glamorous, but they can make for good character building, extra cash, familial contributions, or stories to tell when you're on Jimmy Kimmel one day.
- You don't have to have fancy "my father is the CEO of Olive Garden" connections to find a job. If you've met another person, that is a connection. Talk to everyone about your job hunt. This is useful to keep in mind not just in high school, but always!

- High school jobs can build skills for later in life. If you're babysitting, you could use that to become a full-time nanny, or count it as "experience with children" for any number of jobs. If you're a waiter, you'll have customer service and communications experience forever.

- This is the time in your life you'll probably have the fewest expenses and the most ability to save. Don't waste it if you need it.

GETTING OUT OF THIS ONE-HORSE TOWN

When it came time to apply to colleges, my high school was positively cutthroat, but no one, not even guidance counselors, teachers, and especially not my parents, talked to me about how much higher education was going to cost. Money was my parents' concern, and like my sister said, if they didn't seem worried, then there was nothing to worry about. Something nagged at me, though. I knew my family had financial troubles, but I was too distracted by college app hysteria to look into it. I had wanted to apply everywhere, but it was expensive to submit applications. *Money Magazine* reported in 2017 that college applications cost anywhere from $25 to $90 each. Over the past ten years, the average has gone up from $35 a pop to $40 an application. The average high school senior will spend $1,700 on application fees alone. You're spending a significant amount of money *just* to be evaluated and possibly rejected.

Speaking of which, I was dead-set on Northwestern University in Chicago because I'd heard great things about its journalism school and wanted to attend comedy classes at Second City, the former home of Tina Fey and Amy Poehler. I applied and waited eagerly for my letter. My second choice was Emerson College in Boston, which had a similar price tag to Northwestern of around $40,000 a year (in 2006).

In April, I was accepted at the University of Florida. Florida has two long-standing programs that would have allowed me to go to UF essentially for free: Florida Prepaid, a prepaid, interest-accruing college fund that my parents had been paying into for me, and Bright Futures, a lottery-funded scholarship that allows a student resident who fulfills certain SAT score and community service hour requirements to attend an in-state Florida university for a huge discount. I qualified for Bright Futures. The other benefit was my dad had gone to UF, so I could also be considered for legacy scholarships.

I didn't care about—or fully understand—any of that.

As college acceptances neared, my high school did something I will neither forget nor forgive. The already competitive atmosphere skyrocketed with the placement of a bulletin board near the entrance to the school with every senior's name prominently displayed. Under our name, we were supposed to pin papers with our college acceptances and then a star or check beside the one we'd chosen to go to. Some of the honors kids were smart enough to get into Ivy League schools but took Bright Futures, used their prepaid, and accepted bids from local colleges like UF, Florida State University, or University of Central Florida (whose prestige was rising back then). The less wealthy kids who weren't going to community colleges were accepting spots at Florida International University or Florida Atlantic University, which I always thought of as proof they were driven or smart but just not wealthy enough. Most of those types (honors but not rich) accepted University of Florida's admission because even though it was in state, the school was starting to become "hard to get into."

That was the phrase everyone was enamored with: "hard to get into." It said that you were "good enough to get in" and "good enough to actually go." That could mean you had a scholarship because you were smart or that your parents were smart enough to figure out a way for you to go (student loans, second mortgages, witchcraft).

Every day I looked at that bulletin board to see what kind of person was going out of state and what kind of person was staying in state. It became about more than just college, though. I wrapped my entire mental health and sense of self-worth up with getting into and going to a school outside Florida.

It was a financial soap opera. Years later, when I asked my parents why they allowed me to take out huge student loans to go out of state for college when I could have gone to UF for essentially nothing, they argued that I *needed* to leave Florida. But they weren't being financially realistic. They were, like me and like many other people awaiting college acceptances, acting solely on emotion.

I asked my mom what would have happened had she and my dad said something like, "You need to be realistic about this. You are going to UF. End of discussion." My mom looked appalled at the suggestion: "It was worth every penny for your mental health and for your happiness." Right. But plenty of people probably "need" to get out of their hometowns and can't afford to. It wasn't practical, I said.

"Okay, so it wasn't practical," she replied. Case closed.

My environment at the time was, admittedly, not ideal. My dad was drinking heavily. I was a closeted bisexual in a group of friends who routinely used the word *lesbian* as a pejorative. I don't think anyone thought I was queer, but I stuck out like a sore thumb in a way people couldn't place and didn't like. All I ever talked about in my diary was getting out of Florida and how if I couldn't, I'd kill myself.

This is not a lighthearted joke about suicide. It was a serious consideration. I'd first thought about killing myself in the fourth grade by throwing myself down the stairs in my elementary school. I'd spent most of high school self-harming with a razor blade, and though that's not necessarily a precursor to suicide, it wasn't great. I didn't know how much longer I could hide my sexuality without dire, perhaps fatal, consequences.

So I set my sights on Northwestern University in Chicago: the holy grail. The place that would rescue me at last! I toured the school, met with alumni, went to potential student events, got sweatshirts and shorts—the whole shebang. And then I didn't get in.

After that, I became obsessed with what school *would* go under my name on that board. I have no recollection of why Emerson College was my second choice. It might have been because at the time *The Princeton Review* website labeled it one of the gayest schools in America. As of 2018, it ranks #3 in LGBTQ student body and #7 in Least Religious Students. There was also a scholarship program at Emerson: the Honors Program. If you got in, tuition was half-off with the requirement that you'd take extra classes and write two theses. I got into both Emerson and Honors. Tuition alone was around $37,000 per year in 2006. Now Emerson costs $62,000 per year for room and board, food, other fees, and tuition. I wasn't at all aware of the price tag then, partly because my parents told me that I shouldn't worry about it. They didn't know I was self-harming or queer, but they knew I was miserable in Florida and they thought leaving for college would cure me.

I was desperate and ignorant—a dangerous combination. My mom bristles, but I can only imagine the number of young people who *need* to move and simply cannot make it work financially. (*We* couldn't reasonably make it work financially.) That just makes me both lucky and foolish. In hindsight, a strong money reality check would have been worth a try to avoid future mental health breakdown triggers in the form of $30,000 in loans (which is not even on the high end of student debt for my generation).

Maybe nothing would have deterred me. There's a reason Romeo and Juliet were teenagers. Being impulsive and stubborn can be part of the deal, but it doesn't have to be.

———

In April 2017, I flew to Chicago to meet with seven awesome teenage girls from Gage Park High School. We ate fruit and tacos as soft jazz music played in the classroom, and we talked about their plans for the future.

This school and its students are constantly battling a negative reputation. The second thing that auto-fills when you google "Gage Park High School" is "deaths." According to USNews.com, the school has a 97 percent "economically disadvantaged" population, as they so euphemistically put it. Jessica Aceves, a senior learning program coordinator for Build On, a nonprofit that runs after-school programs in Chicago, said that in 2016, 25 percent of students there went on to college. Gage Park has a 40.3 percent graduation rate, 25.1 percent lower than the Chicago public schools average of 65.4 percent. Most of the houses surrounding the school have wood boarding up the windows.

The young women I interviewed at Gage Park were low income and nonwhite. They were thoughtful and funny. They've seen the mistakes their parents and older siblings have made and don't want to fall into the same traps. They're worried about loans, debt, and getting a good job.

Jasmine wants to be a photographer. College, for her, wouldn't be about education but about making connections. Instead of attending, she thinks she could network around Chicago or make a name for herself on social media. (At the end of the interview, she gave me her Instagram handle, and because I appreciated the hustle, I followed her.)

Of all the students I talked to, Jasmine's classmate Marina will be spending the most money on college, attending a private university. She guessed it'll run her $46,000.

"For what? A piece of paper?" Jasmine cut in, shaking her head in disapproval. (I asked Jasmine if she wanted to write this book instead. She declined.)

Marina said she has some savings from her job at Chipotle

and thinks her parents might kick in some money, but maybe not. A sibling may have ruined that for the both of them by making their parents pay for school, which they eventually dropped out of. Marina disdainfully reports that her sibling lives at home and racks up credit card debt.

Dry, whip-smart Cristina doesn't know what she wants to do with her life yet—but she does know that college, because she doesn't have specific major in mind, isn't for her. She's jaded. She sees colleges as businesses she wants to opt out of.

"I like reading books and stuff but not on something a white man wrote," she said. "I've been doing it up until this grade, and I don't want to continue to do it for another four years." (I love Cristina.)

As Jasmine's and Cristina's experiences highlight, there is no shame in deciding you'd rather save the money, in moving forward in your future a different way, or in not being ready to go to college. I've never believed that you automatically become an adult the day you turn 18. As the wise Jasmine said, "I still have to ask to go to the bathroom, but I'm supposed to know what I want to do with the rest of my life as soon as I walk across the stage?"

Don't keep the money aspect of college a secret, and don't stress prestige over practicality. I was surprised to learn how many of the current high school and college students I talked to had had serious discussions with their parents about paying for school. It was so unlike my own experience. Many said their parents told them frankly that when it came to paying for college, they were on their own. There was no emotional boohooing about it.

The problem is twofold: Parents don't talk to their kids about how they're affording college as a family or about scholarships or about realistic expectations for where they can apply, and kids don't talk to *each other* about what their other plans might be for after high school or if they're attending, about how they're really affording college.

FINANCIAL AID

There are steps we can take to prepare though. Kelly Peeler, founder of NextGenVest, a college financial prep company, told me the stunning news that it's possible to negotiate your college tuition. When I was 18, I would have been terrified. Who wants to be the thorn in your new university's side before you even get there?

Former dean of admissions at Columbia Anna Ivey agreed that the first financial aid package you receive is just a suggestion. It's up to you to fill in any circumstances or changes in income that you think might lower the number. (On the flip side, if your parent landed a new job or you inherited family money, you can turn down loan offers. There's no sense going into debt for something you could pay for interest free.)

I was furious to learn that tuition numbers could fluctuate. I can't imagine the cool-as-hell teen who lights up a cigar and slides the envelope back across the table to NYU's admissions department with a chilly, "No dice." Ivey said unless something massively bad happens, a school isn't going to take away an acceptance once it's been given. So why not negotiate the price?

Choosing a school makes you a consumer paying for a product (education); the cost shouldn't be a mystery or a burden. What can we do? These are Peeler's thoughts:

1. Read your award letter carefully, and look up anything you don't understand. Note what's a grant (aka free money) and what's a loan (which you'll pay to borrow).

2. Understand interest. Your interest rate tells you how much you'll pay each year to borrow the money you're being loaned. Financial aid award letters don't typically show interest rates. (Tricky!)

3. Think ahead when choosing a major. Peeler said a lot of people pick a course of study without looking at the top jobs and starting salaries. It might be a downer to look at the annual salary of say a book editor or journalist (low, guys; it's low), but it might influence your choice.

Ivey said it doesn't help that college admissions are purposely confusing when it comes to finances. Need-blind admission doesn't mean that once accepted, the school will fill in that need. If you're on the margins for admission, your ability to pay tuition may factor in to whether a school can afford to help you attend. (Ivey said rejection is more humane than getting students' hopes up and then not providing the funds for them to attend.) I don't know what's worse: not getting in, getting in and not being able to afford it, or getting in and spending the rest of your life bogged down in debt. All three are common problems.

TAKEAWAYS

- Attaching self-worth to material achievement or to things largely out of your control is not healthy. Making financial decisions based on competitiveness and entitlement can bite you in the ass down the line.
- More debt might be worth it, or it might not. Decide what you're okay with, and look at how much the jobs you are interested in after graduation pay.
- If you don't know what you want to do, maybe chill a second and don't rack up debt you might not need for an education you might not use. There's no rush.

3

THE NECK TATTOO OF THE FINANCIAL WORLD

When my sister was 18, she went into a tattoo parlor and asked for a neck tattoo of a flower. The artist turned her down because she was too young to make a lifelong decision that might affect her ability to work in the future.

Wouldn't it be nice if someone did the same thing for student loans?

Paying for college is marketed as paying for an identity. Think of all the "Harvard Mom" bumper stickers and "UNC Grad 4Ever" T-shirts—the clothing equivalent of neck tattoos you get at 18.

I believed that identity fallacy. So did my sister, who attended a community college in Santa Monica, California, paying out-of-state tuition, when she could have attended the same caliber of school for free at home in Florida.

She ended up coming back to South Florida when she re-

alized Santa Monica was too far away, too expensive, and too
unfamiliar. After living with my parents for a while, she enrolled at Tallahassee Community College (TCC). Two years
later, she transferred to Florida State University (FSU). But
had she just gone straight to TCC from high school, she would
have paid almost nothing for that *and* for her eventual transfer
to FSU. Instead, my sister has $30,000 in loans just like I do
(and I went to a liberal arts college in Boston). The pressure
to go somewhere new, and to do so immediately, got to her too.

As of this writing, my student loans are spread out among
three accounts with different student loan service providers.
They provide customer service, process payments, or help set
up payment plans. Providers are chosen either by you directly
(private) or through the government choosing a company
like Nelnet or Navient as the provider of the loan (federal).

I have two loans I took out directly with Nelnet (National
Education Loan Network) that add up to $4,000, and I have
one with Navient, a student debt collector and servicer spun
off from another loan company, Sallie Mae, that is about
$26,000. (Over the course of writing this book, I paid off the
two smaller Nelnet ones. Go me!) I learned the exact amount
of the loans I had ten years after I took them out. (I take back
that "Go me!") I never looked before that because I assumed
the number was so high that it would be unfathomable to me.
(It is.) I lived my life as if my loans didn't exist while my mom
paid them off in tiny increments. Many people similarly bury
their indebted heads in the loan sand, and a lot of them have
it way worse than my sister and I do.

In his stand-up special "Kid Gorgeous," the comedian
John Mulaney has an incredible joke about his own student

loans. Mulaney, who is in his mid-thirties, railed against paying $120,000 ("in 1999 money!") to major in English and not
read any of the books he was assigned to read. He basically
paid that much to party, he said. "Let's face it," he joked, "if
you've graduated from college and you're still giving money
to your alma mater, you're like a john that's fallen in love with
his prostitute." The entire bit perfectly highlights my own
regrets about paying for school (and the absurdity of colleges
then asking, after graduation for "MORE MONEY!," as he
screamed during his show).

Adriana Ariza, a 25-year-old graduate student at Clare-
mont University in her third year of a developmental psychology degree, had $75,000 in federal loans when I interviewed
her in 2017. She's aiming for a PhD and had three years left
in her program, which takes seven years total.

As a first-generation college student, Ariza didn't have
any guidance from her parents when it came to student loans.
Her father is an immigrant from Mexico. Both her parents
drilled into her that she needed to go to college in the land
of opportunity. In the end, she estimates she'll be $82,000
total in student loan debt, a massive number that takes my
breath away. Within psychology, she explained, you can't get
a decent-paying job with just a bachelor's degree, but fur-
thering your education puts you even more into debt. It's a
financial Ouroboros.

Ariza said she and her friends in similar positions view the
numbers as too outrageous to even think about, so they don't.
And if they do, they believe either the debts will be wiped out
by a nationwide student loan crisis or Ariza thinks maybe
she'll just die with them. *C'est la vie!* (I like this girl.)

In a 2015 article in the *New York Times*, author Lee Siegel admitted that he'd chosen to purposefully default on his student loans. (He faced a ton of controversy for this stance and went on various media outlets to defend himself.) "It struck me as absurd," Siegel wrote, "that one could amass crippling debt as a result, not of drug addiction or reckless borrowing and spending, but of going to college. Having opened a new life to me beyond my modest origins, the education system was now going to call in its chits and prevent me from pursuing that new life, simply because I had the misfortune of coming from modest origins."

Like Ariza following her father's wish for her to "rise above" their immigrant status, Siegel said loans discourage young people from trying to rise above their "lower-middle-class origins" and maintain the wealth status quo using education as leverage. "To my mind, they have learned to live with a social arrangement that is legal, but not moral," he wrote of those paying back their loans. Ariza continues to pay off her loans in small amounts, but she's living paycheck to paycheck like most of her friends. She has immediate concerns like bills and rent to consider.

"If you begin to think about it, it leads to like, a panic attack," she said.

———

Community college, which for many people is free, can be a good financial buffer and a segue into independence. Students I interviewed at Palm Beach State College (a community college in Florida) in 2017 were largely happy with their choice of school. They were all excited to graduate without a lot of (or any!) debt and they felt badly for their peers who had chosen more expensive schools, hoping to be guaranteed better jobs.

Many of these students knew what they wanted to do and that an associate's degree was enough. Some didn't know yet and didn't want to pay for a four-year university just to find out. Many also didn't want to pay for housing, and so they lived at home to save money or to help their parents care for their siblings—wanting to continue contributing to the household rather than becoming a financial drain. Some simply weren't ready to live on their own (and were self-aware about it).

On *Late Night with Seth Meyers* in 2015, Dr. Jill Biden, former Vice President Joe Biden's wife, called community college "the best kept secret in America." The Northern Virginia Community College professor said people judge the education as subpar, but Dr. Biden asserts, "I know differently and so do the millions of people across the country who have received an affordable, quality higher education at community college."

It's not all roses, though. One student at Palm Beach State College said her sister, who attends a private college, berates her for her choice. One said she was afraid to tell her friends. Even Palm Beach itself felt that it needed to up its game: in 2010, it rebranded from Palm Beach Community College to Palm Beach State College. (Some students agreed this actually did make the school more palatable.) But for the most part, the students I spoke with feel grateful they're attending a community college and won't have loans like other people their age.

And if you're so inclined, you can also look into vocational or trade schools, many of whom offer job training for skills like welding and plumbing where people can go on to make six-figure salaries. The stigma and false idea that college indicates excellence and success keeps people for whom this would be a fantastic option from actually pursuing said fantastic option.

Facing money problems after getting a college degree has become all too standard when it doesn't need to be. Even so, among my close friends, no one was willing to go on the record about their parents paying off their loans for them. (I'm mortified my mom was doing it, even if it was behind my back.)

Even Lilly, a currently unemployed American 26-year-old living in Switzerland whom I interviewed, asked that I not use her last name so as not to throw her parents under the bus. (Their friends give them a hard time about paying for their daughter.) She also feels weird about other people knowing. It's one of the biggest stigmas about my generation. How dare we graduate without jobs into a shitty economy and deign to borrow money from our parents to get on our feet! How dare we move back home until we find a job! How dare we let them cover our loans until we are able to do it ourselves (or even accept their paying the loans as a gift if they are able to help us out that way)!

A dual citizen of the United States and Germany, Lilly finished school and moved in with her parents, who are living in Switzerland. Her parents helped her pay for the private university she attended in California and took out loans for her under their name. They also gave her and her brother money to live on after school while they looked for work. Lilly's parents' friends who don't have children themselves point out that Lilly's parents could have spent that money on their own lives: vacations, nicer cars, newer homes. I argued that once you have kids, you should expect to spend more money taking care of them than your friends who don't have kids would spend on someone other than themselves. (My parents are in debt. My aunt and uncle who don't have children drive Mercedes-Benzes.)

———————

According to a survey conducted in 2016 by the credit card company Discover, if a child takes out a student loan, their parents are now more willing to help pay it back than they were just four years earlier (61 percent, up from 55 percent). Half of those parents surveyed in 2016 said that they were "very worried that student debt may affect their child's ability to buy a house, car or other large purchase." A 2016 *Forbes* article, "More Parents Taking On Their Kids' College Debt," cited a University of Southern California study showing that 17 percent of parents "around age 50" are currently paying back their child's student loans. In the last decade or so, the amount that students borrowed in the United States has soared from $3.6 billion to $12 billion. Loans become not only the student's responsibility but a family burden.

Forbes thinks this is because baby boomers and Gen Xers, many of whom are parents and have debt themselves, don't fully understand the risks of cosigning student loans for their millennial or Gen Z kid until it's too late. More than half said the decision negatively affected their own credit scores and caused them to put off their retirement. The other problem is that they're borrowing more for student loans than parents and students in previous generations due to rising college tuition.

According to *U.S. News & World Report*, the average total cost of attending a private university has jumped 157 percent in the last 20 years, while in-state tuition and fees at public national universities have grown the most, increasing 237 percent.

"To put those numbers into perspective," Emmie Martin wrote in a 2017 CNBC article, "a 1988 graduate of Harvard University would have spent $17,100 on tuition during their senior year. Now, in their 50s, they'd have to pay $44,990 in tuition for their child to attend Harvard today."

In 2011, when I was fresh out of college, the *Fiscal Times* reported that parents were depleting their nest eggs by paying their children's rent, food, and cell phone bills after graduation—all of this often on top of paying back loans. Because graduates are often in debt, more parents are also helping their kids buy their first homes, which is seen as an adult rite of passage. "Independent adulthood" can now mean being subsidized by your generous-to-their-own-detriment parents. Meanwhile those without parents who can subsidize it or without parents at all feel "less adult" for not being able to afford the trappings of adulthood.

This problem isn't affecting everyone equally. In 2016, *Forbes* reported that black, college-educated middle- to upper-class parents with more than one child with student debt are most often the ones paying back their children's loans. (Studies have also shown that black parents in the US are more invested in their children's educations because they know they'll need higher degrees to get the same positions and pay as white applicants. Ain't America great?)

John Brunson, a 30-year-old black bartender, is a good example of this. He attended the University of Central Arkansas to study communications and theater. He could make tuition work, but he needed loans to cover housing, books, and living costs. Brunson's father runs Central Arkansas Planning and Development, and his mom is a phlebotomist. Both of them went to school—his dad to college and his mom to training in her field. He said he and his dad talked only a little about loans, but both of his parents were *very* intent on college for him.

John decided to take out a personal loan from Sallie Mae and a federal loan. A student advisor (a version of a guidance counselor at his high school) told him she could find him all the loans he wanted. "Sign here, here, here, here and here," he joked. But John said she never explained any of the loans he was signing up for. He did not fully understand interest rates. And he didn't know that you can't consolidate your loans if your debt has been sold.

That's right! Student loans, if they're private, can be sold to debt collection agencies and banks you never took loans from. John said some of his loans have been sold off so many times that he'll just get a random letter in the mail from a bank he's never heard of saying, "Hey, you owe us $9,000."

"I'll try to contact them and be like, 'Well, what is this debt in reference to?' They can't tell you. They don't know," he said.

On his illuminating late-night show *Last Week Tonight*, John Oliver elaborates on this phenomenon. In a segment called "Debt Buyers," Oliver explains that delinquent debts (over ninety days late) have given birth to a whole industry of outside companies buying debt from banks and other lenders, creating a debt maze. Banks are selling off debt to create more money for more loans, and then these debt-buying companies can come after *you* because you now owe *them* money. So you may have taken out a loan with Bank of America, but by the time you pay it back, you have no idea who you're paying, which is what's happening to our buddy John Brunson.

The information being sold isn't always truthful. It can get shuffled around or lost or change hands many times, and the debt buyers don't check if they have it right before they come to collect. (And if you're not on top of it? You could pay a loan off TWICE.)

"Some [debt collectors] work within the boundaries of the law," John Oliver warned on his show. But others will call your house, your family members, your employer, leave threatening voicemails, or tell consumers that if they can't pay they should kill themselves. Debt buyers also disproportionately come after people in black or Latino neighborhoods, according to the Human Rights Watch. Oliver reported that the debt buyers can legally sue people (which they do a lot). When 95 percent don't show up for their court dates, the debt buyer wins by default and can garnish the indebted person's wages—again, all legally. None of this has happened to John Brunson yet, but he expects it is coming in his future. "It's all a tangled confused web now," he said.

He knows he should pay the loans off, but all told, if he paid the amount he needed to every month to be able to pay it off in a timely fashion, it'd be more than his rent. (Insert panic attack here, as Ariza said.)

So what about consolidating your loans? Federal Student Aid defines consolidating as "[combining] multiple federal education loans into one loan. The result is a single monthly payment instead of multiple payments." Before you consolidate, you have to ask your student loan service provider if you qualify. The loans have to be direct federal loans—and not yet sold the way Brunson's have been. Consolidation can make your life easier, but it can also negatively affect your credit or give you a higher interest rate than your existing loans. You may forfeit your loan forgiveness eligibility too.

It's hard to say definitively what any one person with loans should or shouldn't do. "If anybody ever gives you a one-size-fits-all solution, you can immediately disregard what they said and know that they don't know what they're talking about," loan consolidation expert Jan Miller warned me. It's all a mess. For example, Miller said, people in medical school graduate and ultimately have to decide if they want to go into private practice or the nonprofit sector. These decisions will influence how quickly and how much of their income can go toward paying off the loans they took out—like Adriana Ariza's situation.

Choosing nonprofit work can qualify a person for forgiveness programs, but they should research specifically what the forgiveness numbers are before thinking they can rely on that instead of a high-paying private sector job. There's also loan deferment, which in some circumstances means you can halt paying loans and not accrue interest like you might with a forgiveness program.

According to the Department of Education's student loan division, you may be able to defer your loan repayments if you are:

- Enrolled in an approved rehabilitation training program for the disabled community

- Experiencing economic hardship while serving in the Peace Corps
- Unemployed or unable to find full-time employment
- A parent

But there are many more beyond these, so go to the Federal Student Aid Office website and poke around. There are also student loan forgiveness programs if you've done volunteer work, have been in the military, or practice medicine in certain communities.

TAKEAWAYS

- Student loan debt is consuming a lot of people's lives, in every generation. Knowing you're not alone in your misery should eliminate some stigma and galvanize you to work toward national student loan forgiveness policy and a better future for all students.
- There are ways to get forgiveness if your debt is so huge and inconceivable that you feel that you could never afford to pay it all.
- If you can afford to pay it off faster, you'll end up paying less overall (because of interest).

4

LEGALIZED EVIL

During my sophomore year of college, in 2007, I moved out of the dorms and into a shared house in Boston's Allston neighborhood. The duplex I lived in with my two roommates rented for $1,500 total (which is typically the rent cost for one person where I live now in LA. Ugh.) My portion was $500. We had very little furniture, and the floors were always sticky for no discernible reason.

Like in high school, I saved no money at all in college, but I don't remember spending that much money either. My loans and my scholarship were covering my tuition, and the biggest expenses were textbooks and beer. (That might explain the sticky floors, actually.) Everything my group of friends did was very cheap, and we prided ourselves on that. I had a job almost the whole time I was in college, working as a paid intern for the *Boston Globe* where I made $1,000 a month, half of which went toward my rent. I got the gig at the *Globe* through my unpaid work at Emerson's college newspaper, the *Berkeley Beacon*. I don't remember a time during my freshman year that I wasn't either in class or working in the *Beacon*'s basement offices. I was determined to climb up the ranks and eventually become editor-in-chief my senior year. If it interfered with the *Beacon*—study-abroad opportunities, relationships, hobbies, homework—it was gone.

When it came time to apply for the job at the *Globe*, we *Beacon* staffers had to compete not only with each other, but also with newspaper staffs from schools all around Boston, at places like Northeastern, Suffolk, and Harvard. There were four shifts on the news desk. In my interview with the *Globe* editors, hoping no one would want it and it would allow me to more easily land the position, I said it was my dream to have the late-night crime reporting slot (6:00 p.m.–2:00 a.m.).

I got it.

I worked every weeknight. I was often given a car and a police radio. I drove around Boston talking to cops and the families of murder victims and people whose homes had just burned down. It was an insanely stressful and tiring—but rewarding—job. I was competing with everyone in my life: my friends were reporters, my boyfriend was a reporter, my enemies were reporters. The *Globe* benefited immensely from these young and hungry interns working all hours for low salaries, but I didn't see it that way. I couldn't believe I was even allowed in the hallowed *Globe* newsroom AND that they were paying me, even if the money didn't compensate me for working overtime and weekends trying to get more clips and bylines.

As long as I could pay my rent, I didn't really care about where the rest of my newspaper salary went. Because the *Globe* money was for an internship, they didn't have us put anything into a 401(k) and I had no other retirement plans (not that I knew what those were yet). The *Globe* took taxes out of the paycheck, and that was it. The rest was mine, and sometimes I even got a tax refund check at the end of the year. Even with all that cushion, it wouldn't have occurred to me to start a savings account (which, oh my god, you should do in college if you can. Why didn't I do that?? Why didn't I know I could do that?).

I don't remember any of my friends talking about saving or having savings. I don't remember any authority figure telling me to save money. I basically never thought about money until I really, really needed it. I was way more concerned with career advancement than with payment.

One of the biggest fights I kept getting into with my dad when I was in college went something like this:

Me: Dad! I got published in my first national print
        publication. This is a huge deal because it's my
        dream and also I'm just twenty years old.
Dad: That's wonderful! How much are they paying
        you?

For someone with such a loose handle on his own finances, my dad consistently brought up payment whenever I made any strides in my career. I railed against this, seeing his constant first question as insulting. That was literally the last thing I cared about. I wanted the eyeballs on my writ-

ing. Contacts to new editors. Bylines in prestigious publications so I could get my next byline in the next prestigious
publication.

It was about the optics of appearing successful. The money
was the part no one saw, so who cared what I was getting
paid? Some of these places, I would have skinned myself and
paid them in my own flesh to be able to write for them.

The question embarrassed me because often I was so excited about being published that I didn't want to mar the oc-
casion by talking payment. I'd sometimes forget to ask the
publications. I found it to be a huge buzzkill. But if my dad
eventually wanted to ask me about what I was being paid
later on in the conversation? I shouldn't have been so hard-
line about it. The truth is that I was embarrassed I hadn't
even thought about it.

———————

So how *do* you navigate spending and saving in college? Admissions consultant Anna Ivey said she worries that more
and more students are picking colleges based on fun and
amenities rather than education—and this results in overspending on drinking, Greek life, and other socializing with
new, exciting friends. That's not to say you should hole up
in your dorm and never hang out, just that that's not all
college is about. And being too into that aspect can lead to
poor finances at a time when you're already spending on
textbooks, extracurriculars, and dorm furnishings, let's say.
Though for textbooks, I imagine that if you're a college
student, you've already figured out that you don't need to

get them all before class begins and that you don't need to get them new or from anywhere other than the library. I can't tell you how many times a professor insisted we get a textbook, only for us never to use it. I also had roommates who were older than me and in the same major, so I got a lot of hand-me-downs. (I even wore my ex-girlfriend's old graduation robe.)

Studies show the majority of college students work part-time during school, and most of them work in the service industry. (A 2013 survey in *Seventeen* magazine said American students average nineteen hours of work a week on top of school, and most don't make enough to pay any of their tuition, relying still on student loans and scholarships.) Finding a job in college can be similar to finding one in high school, only now you may have a longer résumé and are over 18. This means you have more paths open to you—you can legally bartend, for one. Bartending requires taking a class and getting a mixology certification. Some of these classes can cost $200 to $500, though some have special deals available. Usually these classes are spread out and run forty hours. There are different schools with different levels of credibility. Bartending can be a good job during college, but the income isn't stable. Plus, my sister, who worked as a waitress at a bar, said it kept her out late hours. That's hard when you also have classes.

My girlfriend currently works at her college, which also gives her a discount on tuition. Some graduate students work as teaching assistants for the same reason. She manages a building, working during the day and taking mostly night classes when she can. This has been great for having a job during school and for not having to travel far for class, but it's a bit stressful because it's a full-time job while being a full-time student.

I was lucky to be one of the small number of people who had a part-time job in college that was in the field I wanted to go into. But pursuing my ideal career path led to some tough financial decisions.

———

The summer before senior year, I landed my dream internship at *The Daily Show with Jon Stewart* in New York City.

The internship was organized through the show's parent company Viacom, which encompasses networks like VH1, Comedy Central, and MTV. I was obsessed with *The Daily Show* and with Mr. Stewart—so much so that for my 18th birthday, my mom wrote to him using an address she'd found online (probably that of his manager) and he'd sent back a personalized signed photo, which hung in my bedroom for years. An essay I'd written about my aspiration to work for the show had been published in a 2006 anthology of the best writing by high school students. Being offered this internship was the pinnacle of my life's work. I had to take it.

But money, as always, was an issue. The internship was unpaid. This confused me. I'd never encountered an unpaid job before. Ross Eisenbrey of the Economic Policy Institute said "glamorized" industries started offering unpaid internships because in an economic recession, where young people are desperate for work or for upwardly mobile positions, these industries realized they could now get "quality people for nothing." In 2014, *Forbes* reported that the National Association of Colleges and Employers found that from the mid-1980s to the mid-2000s, the number of college graduates participating in at least one internship rose from "less than 10 percent to over 80 percent." Just 37 percent of students who do an unpaid internship reported that it led to a job offer, only 2 percent higher than students who did no internships at all. Was it worth it?

I grappled with potentially turning down *The Daily Show* and instead staying in Boston for the summer working at my paid internship at the *Globe.* My parents were so disappointed I'd even consider telling Viacom no. They knew how much it would mean to me to work for *The Daily Show,* and the doors putting *TDS* on my résumé could potentially open. It was 2009, just after Barack Obama had been elected, and politics was cool again. All eyes were on *The Daily Show* now. Jon Stewart was a rock star. There was no *Full Frontal with Samantha Bee* yet. No indie political talk shows on YouTube. No satirical news podcasts. Stewart was THE GUY.

The internship was for college credit only, and while I could sublet my place in Boston for the summer, I'd need to find a similarly inexpensive apartment in New York City to funnel that rent money into. The real estate market in Manhattan and the one in the Allston neighborhood of Boston where I lived are not, it turns out, remotely comparable. I'd be bleeding money the entire summer. Still, I wanted to work for Comedy Central, a network I'd stayed up late watching all through high school.

There was also another problem: I was a journalism student, and Emerson didn't consider working for Comedy Central, even the network's political talk show, to be journalism. Since it wasn't an internship within my major, Emerson declined to give me college credit to do it. I couldn't do the internship for pay, and I couldn't do it for credit.

The only option would be to enroll in another school for the summer and get credit there to transfer to Emerson. Emerson would likely reject the credits, but Viacom could feel good knowing it was technically "paying" me, and Emerson could feel good that the internship was benefiting my education. I could enroll for the summer at South Florida's Broward Community College and transfer the credits to Emerson in the fall. I'd be paying BCC money to attend for the summer classes that were my internship. Viacom benefited from my free work, and Broward Community College benefited from my tuition dollars when I wasn't actually a student. It wasn't just an unpaid internship; it was an internship I was paying for.

This is not an uncommon plight. *Inside Higher Ed* published a story in May 2016 about students who *pay* to take unpaid internships and the other unexpected costs of requiring students to take academic internships to graduate. I luckily didn't need an internship other than the *Globe* to graduate, but some programs would have left me no choice.

I eventually accepted the position with *The Daily Show* and had two weeks to search for a suitable person to sublet my Allston apartment and a new place in NYC. A friend took my room in Boston for the summer, and I found a room through Craigslist in Brooklyn, in the Greenpoint neighborhood, where it would take me an hour to get into the city. The rent was $900. I had no idea how I was going to make it through the summer, but I started the internship on my 21st birthday with $2,700 of rent weighing on my shoulders.

In Boston, I was used to working long hours, but with the bright light of a paycheck at the end of the week's tunnel. This was not the case now. College credit wasn't going to pay for my MetroCards or my lunches.

My new place in Brooklyn didn't have a bed frame or any furniture in it, but I didn't have the means to furnish it, so my mattress remained on the floor. My clothes were folded in my suitcase as I'd brought them. Every day for lunch, I went to a bodega and bought a salad buffet and then tried to fill it with as much protein or veggies as I could. A favorite trick was to hide hard-boiled eggs under the lettuce and hope the cashier wouldn't charge me for them.

Spending money is an expected part of living in New York City, but of course there's no travel or clothing stipend given during most unpaid internships. You live far away from the office to avoid paying high rent, and then your commute costs you time and money. Now that I was working in a TV production office (and not as a grungy nighttime crime reporter), I needed new clothes that didn't have spaghetti stains on them. I needed button-downs, pencil skirts, and nice pants. I'd try and get them cheap from less expensive places, but the shirts were so poorly made they always ripped under the armpits if I moved the wrong way or unraveled at the seams as I made coffee runs. I never looked as good as the other interns, and I worried my bosses saw me as sloppy because of it.

Stealing clothing became a constant fantasy. I'd look in the windows of stores and wonder if I could just bargain with the salesperson for some kind of discount. I imagined having invisibility powers, the ability to walk in and walk out with ten usable work skirts. In a particularly rough moment, I actually did try to shoplift a skirt from one popular retail chain. There was a branch of the store in downtown Manhattan that I'd sometimes go into to torture myself. I'd walk around looking at all the clothing and jewelry I couldn't afford, telling myself it wasn't emotional cutting; I was just seeing what was trendy to try and re-create at cheaper stores later.

This particular day, I was so overwhelmed that I became angry with the store itself. How dare it get to decide what I could and could not have? Its prices were a personal attack on me and people like me. If I stole something, I'd be doing everyone a favor.

I walked out with the skirt. And I was immediately caught.

The security guard called me back, pulled the skirt out of my purse, and asked where the receipt was. I didn't have a receipt, and I acted surprised the skirt had somehow fallen into my small purse. He started to walk me back into the store, but I left the skirt in his hands and took off running. I ran for blocks, tears streaming down my face.

This was a new low. This was desperation. I had to admit to myself that financially, things were not just bad; they were crushing me. My health was declining, and I was doing shit that was impulsive. What good would it do to put *The Daily Show* on my résumé if I'd also have to add a shoplifting conviction? Winona Ryder was an icon, but I wasn't looking to copy her downward spiral. (Although, wow, S*tranger Things*! What a comeback!)

I needed to make extra money during this internship. My

first idea was to get another job, but my long hours at the internship left my weekdays unusable. I put my résumé in at a few restaurants, but all replied that they needed people on weekdays. I had no retail experience, so those places never even called me. Looking back, I could have maybe found a babysitting gig, but I didn't know any families in the city. I thought about asking to cut my internship hours down so I could get a second job, but I also thought about the other interns working harder than me and how that would look. When it came time for recommendations or for hiring full-time, I didn't want to be "the slacker."

My next idea was to pawn my belongings. I had some jewelry that my aunt and grandmother had given me. I was nervous about what I'd say when they eventually asked why I never wore the pieces, but I thought that was a problem for future Gaby. I had a pair of iPod speakers and an alarm clock. That Saturday, I put together bags of clothes and old comic books and went to pawnshops to hock the rings and speakers. I went around to consignment shops like Buffalo Exchange and Crossroads trying to resell my clothing.

The pawnshops took the rings, but left me with the speakers. They stayed heavy in the brown paper bags as I walked around trying to get someone to buy the clothes.

Selling your clothing to a thrift store is a particularly cruel brand of humiliation. First, you wait in line with a bunch of other people, avoiding looking each other in the eye or wondering what kind of bad life choices led all of you to be waiting for this chance to be rejected.

Let's say you paid $50 for a dress and wore it once. Chloe from Buffalo Exchange will look at it sideways and offer you

$1 for it. I never made significant cash selling my clothing, but I always came back for more abuse. A lot of it was also me trying prove Derek and his mustache wrong about my tweed jacket collection.

Selling my clothing was a bust on that day too. I think I made $8 on clothing I'd spent $80 on originally. One bag remained full of sad, useless clothes, and the other held the iPod speakers no one wanted. Both arms full, I walked down the hot Manhattan street, devastated and embarrassed.

The bags broke, of course. The handles ripped off the brown paper. The speaker fell onto the street, and a piece flew off. The clothes spilled out onto where people had spit and peed and fornicated. It was garbage, and I was garbage too. I sat down on the sidewalk and leaned against a building, my knees to my chest, and cried. It was gross, but I was too sad to care. And because it was New York City, no one else cared either.

I did not know what to do. I had an account in the red, and I'd never applied for a credit card before. The idea terrified me. I wouldn't get one for another couple of years. I made up my mind to leave my internship to go back to Florida and stay with my parents. There, I could collect the money from my sublet Allston apartment and try to get my bank account back in the black.

This is what should have happened. This could have, in hindsight, been the straw that broke the camel's back and the way for me to finally clean up my act.

What happened instead was that I called my grandmother and cried. Meme agreed to pay my rent for one month, buying me a month of scrounging up the amount for the next month's rent, which I did with some freelance blogging gigs and a bit more success selling clothing at different outlets.

At the time, I was so grateful to her for covering for me so I could stay in New York and finish my internship. But the experts call what she did that day "enabling." And it was enabling that allowed me to get by paycheck to paycheck without doing anything substantial to fix my life for years to come. I didn't have to start handling money differently. Whenever it seemed that there was no hope, some kind of "miracle" would happen to keep me afloat for another few days. This might seem like a good thing, but in the long term, it wasn't. I needed to fall to get back up.

For example: When I was 15, my alcoholic dad crashed his car on the highway. He had an empty bottle of Crown Royal under his seat. The EMTs loaded him into the back of the ambulance, and for a reason he can't remember (and that I suspect was white privilege), he was never charged with a DUI. Years later, I said something offhand about how lucky he was to walk away from that night without jail time. He said he wasn't lucky. Getting away with driving drunk had only further convinced him of his own infallibility. It had just been another close call in a long series of close calls he thought of as "daily life." "The lucky addicts go to jail or rehab," he'd said. "Because then they have to stop." I don't fully agree with that statement, but I understand what he meant by it.

On the other hand, my fellow interns were also "enabled" to thrive by *their* relatives of a certain socioeconomic class— likely much more so than my grandmother's bailout of one month's rent. Part of me thinks I should have gone home and learned a hard lesson. The other part is glad I was there to represent non-rich kids at internships. Peter Sterne, who created the popular transparency website Who Pays Interns? has observed that not paying interns creates a racial and economic barrier to the jobs later available.

Sterne, a Columbia University graduate, was inspired by Manjula Martin's transparency site, Who Pays Writers? He went looking for a similar site that would tell him what internships were worth applying for if you were a lower-income person. When he couldn't find one, he made his own. I asked if the companies cared that he was consolidating the information into a shaming website, and Sterne said no. They remarkably don't see a problem with offering unpaid internships. They feel untouchable in this arena: Have your little website! It won't change the number of people who apply here! We have the power!

"Because all or most prestigious media internships are not paid, it weeds out the working class," Sterne said. This results in interns and future employees "who are wealthy and middle class and overwhelmingly white." "If you don't pay your interns," he continued, "that is at odds with this desire to increase diversity."

Eisenbrey of the Economic Policy Institute echoes my experience by pointing out that unpaid interns still have to "dress professionally, and pay for transportation. If you're not from at least the middle class, maybe the upper middle class, forget it," he said.

This was also the experience of Kayla Chenault, a 24-year-old African American graduate student at Eastern Michigan University who did three unpaid internships during her graduate and undergraduate education. When I interviewed her in the of summer 2017, she was doing an internship and working two jobs. "A lot of doubling up on having work and then responsibilities for an internship," she sighed. One unpaid internship involved social media work for a self-published author for college credit.

At first, she felt it was all worth it. "I need to do this if I'm going to advance," she thought. "I had to slog through things in order to get someplace."

But she soon found she was at the mercy of the quirks of this nonpaying employer. Did he want to put her name on her work? Up to him. Did he want to give her references or help her make connections? Up to him. There was no guarantee or protection.

This blows.

In some undergraduate departments like hers (English), it was strongly encouraged (but not required) that students do an unpaid internship. In other departments (for example, the chemistry department), unpaid internships were mandatory to graduate. And then—this is fucked up—Kayla said there was the opportunity to do a special course with an internship in which a student could negotiate for payment from her boss for work like creating a website or writing a book, but then the payment goes to the school. "[The school] gets the money that they would have paid to you if you were a freelancer," she explained.

This is technically legal, if not ethical. And it's definitely bullshit.

Kayla also told me she suffered physical symptoms of stress from her internship. She cried. She felt tokenized, often the only black woman in a room of white interns and used to show donors and parents that the organization is "diverse." She wondered: *Why was I hired? Was it because you saw something in me, or was it because you saw something in my blackness?* I have felt this way too as a queer woman. If you are any kind of minority, then your job is also helping the company find others like you to hire or answering questions about being that minority.

When I worked at Buzzfeed, for instance, my job was being a video creator, but it was also spearheading queer events, answering questions straight people had about queer content, and making content related only to my queerness. Your job is your job, and then you have a second job: professional minority. Unpaid internships can have this insidious consequence, requiring additional labor from minorities, also without compensation.

———

When I graduated, I tried desperately to get coffee with every person who I'd worked with in the hopes that they'd hire me back. They met with me, and it was awkward because it was clear what I wanted. There was no immediate job offer as a result of having interned at *The Daily Show*. Now, do I know for sure that the job I later landed at the *Huffington Post* after graduation wasn't offered to me because it said "Comedy Central" on my résumé? I don't know. I'm not sure how much it made my résumé stand out. So could it have been the best thing I ever did and I'll never know because I wasn't in the room for hiring decisions? Sure.

When you're young and broke and trying to carve your way in the world, every opportunity seems like it's do-or-die. Looking back, I'm not sure how I could have convinced younger me that older me didn't really *need* to work for *The Daily Show*.

And in my new-age spirit, I don't want to discredit any experiences I had that led me to this point. If I hadn't cried about money on that New York sidewalk, would I have made the financial podcast that led to this book? It's maybe naive to think, "It's all leading somewhere," in that "wherever you are is where you're meant to be" destiny way. But it's hard to escape my hippie roots.

SHOULD YOU DO AN UNPAID INTERNSHIP?

Not all companies are shitty about internships. It's easy to find out who with just a little Internet sleuthing at places like Sterne's website and others.

Carolyn D'Anna is the head of human resources at Cohn-Reznick, which was listed as #3 on CNBC's 2017 list of top ten places to intern. The company pays interns $23 per hour, according to Glassdoor (which also provides transparency for salaries).

The reason the public accounting firm offers a paid internship, she said, is that CohnReznick is going to be directly making money off those interns because they are billing clients by the hour and interns spend time working with those same clients. They believe interns should get a cut of that billed time. But there's another reason D'Anna thinks paying interns benefits any company: diversity, just as Sterne said.

D'Anna, who in 2004 started the CohnReznick women's program and now serves on the firm's diversity inclusion initiative council, said CohnReznick's 150 interns are often paying their way through school and would struggle unduly by taking an unpaid internship. She said they've seen that an intern's work ethic drastically changes for the better when they can afford to be interning.

The ones who can't afford their unpaid internships have begun fighting back. According to the *Huffington Post*, in 2015 my former employer Viacom paid $7.2 million to 12,500 former interns across their networks in a class action lawsuit. The suit was filed in 2013, so I missed the cut by four years. It alleged, as I do, that the work was comparable to that of employees. The Viacom internship now pays. In a 2013 class action lawsuit, unpaid interns on the Darren Aronofsky film *Black Swan* sued Fox Searchlight over their poor treatment on that film. But labor attorneys have historically had trouble finding people willing to jeopardize their career by suing their first employer, which makes sense.

———

Eisenbrey said he believes unpaid internships give employers the idea that you're desperate. For instance, when someone applies for a job with multiple unpaid internships, he says it tells him that "the employer didn't take them as seriously" and "that they're willing to work for nothing. Therefore, I can give them a lower salary offer than I would someone who had worked a real job, or an internship where they were paid."

I brought up my theory that even if I didn't get hired at *The Daily Show* directly after my internship, having the show on my résumé may have piqued future employers' interests in me. Maybe it made them take a second look at my résumé in the pile. Eisenbrey said there're no data to support that. The only worth an internship has for your future is if you're actually learning something useful. That is, it's an educational internship (like at CohnReznick, perhaps) and not one where you're picking up dry cleaning or getting coffee, no matter how prestigious the employer. And educational internships, he said, are rare. You're much better off applying for paying jobs than for unpaid internships. "Don't sell yourself short. Try and get a real job that pays a decent wage," he said.

This is just one lawyer's opinion. But it's such a complex decision when you're a young person making it. A big reason not to do an unpaid internship, in my opinion, would be to show companies that having unpaid internships won't get them great interns (like you). That's a noble long-game and requires selflessness. For example, the main complainant in the *Black Swan* suit, Eric Glatt, was 42 years old and had enough money that he knew he could do the internship, see what the conditions really were, and then sue to try and make things better for all interns. But not everyone can be like him.

It's hard for me to tell you not to do an unpaid internship when I did one—even though it caused my finances (and psyche) deep damage and furthered my belief that offering them later creates a very narrow, white/upper-class employee pool, which does not benefit any company. I *would* absolutely advise you not to pay for college credits from another university so you can hemorrhage money on an unpaid internship. That was not smart of me. What I can tell you is:

BE OPEN-MINDED. My first mistake was being so dead set on one specific place to intern and basing all my self-worth on its prestige. If you're more open-minded, you won't feel that one offer is do-or-die, the way I did about *The Daily Show*. It's not like I spent all summer becoming Jon Stewart's best friend. Don't get too lost in the clouds about what the internship might look like before you've even arrived at the office.

DON'T BELIEVE THAT YOUR ENTIRE CAREER BEGINS AND ENDS WITH THIS INTERNSHIP. Have multiple options in your back pocket. One could be this unpaid internship: you want to see if you can make it work. One could be a paid internship somewhere else. One could be finding a paying gig in retail or as a lifeguard for the summer so you have more money to spend on your passion projects during the school year. One could be looking for a gig as a counselor on a traveling summer program like Teen Tours or Birthright (I'm *so* Jewish) so you can work for money AND get to see the world. If I'd been more open to other options (like staying in Boston for the summer or looking for a paid job near my parents' house in sunny Fort Lauderdale), I could have avoided a lot of stress and spent less cash.

TAKEAWAYS

- Get a job in college! Have some money coming in so you're not just losing cash for four years. And go to your classes! You wouldn't pay for guac and then just shovel dry chips into your mouth. Get the full college experience (education FOREMOST).

- Unpaid internships are a bad idea if there's a paid alternative. But if there's no way to get paid experience and the job you want requires more experience than you have, that may be the only way forward. But don't do it if it's going to cause irreparable financial harm.

- To make sure we have the best, most diverse workforce, all internships should be paid.

5

THE MILLENNIAL MYTH

After graduating from college with serious debt, I applied for many jobs I was not qualified for. Now that I wasn't in school, I wanted the *Boston Globe* to hire me full time, and they'd made clear they weren't into that idea. Even if they wouldn't hire you, you could still come in and work as many part-time shifts as your schedule allowed, *but* you were technically still freelancing. There were a couple of older guys working there who were still doing the same desk work as us recent grads, hoping to get hired. No one wanted to be them, so everyone worked there a little and applied to other jobs a lot.

First, I hit up an old college professor about a job at the *Boston Business Journal* making Flash animations, something I barely knew how to do. My prospects there seemed good, but I knew that if I got the job, I'd be spending most of my time convincing myself (and my bosses) I wasn't hired as a mistake. Before I even knew if I got that job, I stubbornly moved back to New York instead. I was determined to turn my unpaid struggles at *The Daily Show* into a full-time gig either at Comedy Central or somewhere else in the city. I was desperate to convince myself it had all been worth it. (This was when I tried for coffee with all my old Viacom bosses, which ended up being a dead end.)

It was December 2009. I was living outside the city on my brother and his wife's couch. I applied for jobs at every publication in New York. The days turned to weeks of rejections. Everyone suggested I hit up anyone I had ever met. I reached out to college alumni I found in the Emerson newsletter, people I knew from the high school newspaper job, and my dad's AA acquaintances. I emailed friends of friends, people Meme had met once at the nail salon, a distant cousin my dad heard lived in New York, his old college professor, a circus clown my friend's uncle roomed with in college. These might be slight exaggerations, but you get it: None of those emails or calls led to anything.

In February 2010, I found my first job at Moviefone, later bought by the *Huffington Post*, through AOL Entertainment's job listings website. I was hired to do some short celebrity phone interviews, funny lists about old movies, and various news posts about show business. It was a far cry from the Watergate-breaking reporter I thought I'd be. I'm still not sure why they hired me.

———

While I worked my day job at the *Huffington Post*, I decided to start a side project. I wanted to be a news journalist, and what I was doing wasn't going to get me there. I remember thinking one night, and I don't know what inspired the thought, but it's something I carry with me even now: "To be able to do the thing you want, you have to already be doing it." It doesn't make sense to sit at an entertainment writing job and wish you were an investigative reporter. No one is going to know that's what you really want to do or hand that to you from where you currently are. You have to show them you're already doing it, so they can hire you to do it for them.

So while I was home in Florida for a visit in 2010, I sat in my teenage bedroom and started a blog. This blog is what would eventually launch the career I have today. It was called *100 Interviews*. I decided to launch my blog on Tumblr, a new platform at the time. The goal was simple: interview 100 people in one year. I made a list of types of people I wanted to interview—"someone who survived Hurricane Katrina," "a professional skateboarder," "someone who works at NASA"—and then I committed to finding those people and writing up interviews with them on the blog. It was a massive undertaking.

The blog started out slowly; then one day it got written up in the *Village Voice*. I've searched for years for the person who did the write-up because it didn't have a byline and no one has ever come forward, even though I've promised the person a swift kiss on the mouth. (This might be why they're in hiding.)

After that little article, the blog gained followers. I'd never had followers before, and with that came eyeballs suddenly counting on me to finish the project. What had started as a little idea to keep me busy while I worked my first job became another full-time job and something people were actually expecting a conclusion from. I was MAXIMUM stressed out. My boyfriend at the time helped. My buddies helped. Facebook friends found me interviewees. Other interviewees linked me to more interviewees. Some of the people were nice. Some were very not nice. It was a crapshoot of strangers.

At the buzzer before my self-imposed deadline, I finished the project. I was also still working my full-time job. This project had netted me zero dollars, but it had gained me a little following and some respect on the Internet. (Such currency!) After it was done, I was approached by a small-time literary agent. I was thrilled. I thought my time had finally come. (I was 23. Relax, Gaby.) I was going to have a book! This had been my lifelong ambition ever since I'd won a blue ribbon at the Broward County Fair for my short story "My Very Bad Day!" (I have not changed at all.)

I wrote a proposal for a book based on the *100 Interviews* project. We shopped it around. Everyone passed. The agent stopped emailing me. I'd ruined my shot. (Relax, Gaby.) I went back to focusing on my day job, but AOL was suffering and my coworkers kept getting fired all around me. I was worried I'd be next.

Just to see if I could do it, I wrote a script for an original sitcom pilot based on my college friends. It was NOT GOOD. I mean, it was fine for a first attempt. I went to my Tumblr, where I knew from Google Analytics that I had 25,000 people who'd been reading the *100 Interviews* project. I wrote a post asking if anyone worked in Hollywood. If they did and they were a fan of my writing, would they be interested in reading a script I'd written? It was a bold move. Someone I no longer talk to mocked me for it at the time, calling the post "so desperate and tacky" to my face.

But it worked. An agent from the talent agency Gersh, based in LA, emailed me asking to read my script. He later became my first Hollywood agent. Another man, who worked in some capacity for Nickelodeon, also wanted to read it. (Four years later, that same guy gave me a job writing on a children's sketch show, my first TV writing gig.) Again, the script wasn't good, but it was a start. The point was to show people I was already doing the thing.

I wasn't ready to jump from journalism to show business yet, but I quit my job at *Huffington Post* because I had enough name recognition to start freelancing for blogs, magazines, and newspapers full time. That worked for a while until I ran out of money. I applied for full-time work all over and eventually took a job in IT at a women's health magazine. I was as unqualified for this job as I would have been for the Flash animation job in Boston—maybe even more unqualified. I was constantly googling what I needed to do or watching YouTube tutorials to learn. I cried every lunch hour. My bosses were catching on to my being unable to do this job. After much more crying and deliberating and guilt over giving up a good-paying job with health benefits, I quit and went back to the scrappy life of freelancing. I did that for a few months until I landed a gig (lower pay and no health insurance) at a popular millennial feelings dump blog, *Thought Catalog*.

I wrote a million articles for *Thought Catalog* over the year I worked there. It gained me even more of a fan base, but no retirement savings or long-term career guarantees. The turnover rate at all these little start-up blogs was high. I joined Twitter and tweeted my articles, which gained me a following of about 10,000 people. (Not bad.) I ended up leaving *Thought Catalog* to take a better-paying job at the *Daily Dot*, a news blog that also afforded me health insurance. When I look back on my years in NYC, I took no time off and had no hobbies. All my friends were from work. There was no 9-to-5. Work happened all night, every weekend. I can't remember a time when I wasn't working.

My friends never stopped working either. Far from lazy, we were all stressed, overworked, and underpaid. And we could still barely afford to exist.

———

The first thought people have about my generation, the millennials, is that we're "entitled" or "spoiled." Our mascots are the often tone-deaf Mark Zuckerberg or Hannah Horvath from HBO's *Girls*—out-of-touch rich white liberal arts majors who whine on their iPhones in mommy and daddy's Manhattan pied-à-terre. But those in poverty don't just skip from age 40 to age 3. I identify as a millennial because I was born in 1988, not because I believe we're all alike. For one thing, we don't all have the same experiences surrounding money. In between all the stereotypes are the forgotten: poor and working-class millennials.

Nona Willis Aronowitz, a friend and fellow reporter, has spent the past five years covering working-class millennials and poverty because she became frustrated by publications run by baby boomers publishing stories with photos of young people absentmindedly taking selfies or staring at themselves in the mirror.

One example: *Time* magazine's controversial "ME ME ME Generation" 2013 cover story struck her as particularly out of touch, postrecession. The story presented millennials in a limited way—as solely upper middle class.

"Actual working-class millennials, in the media, are not portrayed as millennials at all," she said in a phone interview. "They're just portrayed as poor people."

This is key. The generational term largely excludes people of color, lower-class people, young people from areas in the South and Midwest ("Real America"), and those who are all three. Are you really going to sit on your East Coast upper-class baby boomer high horse and call a Latinx 25-year-old low-income, single mother working two minimum wage jobs in rural Texas "lazy" or "entitled"?

Aronowitz didn't pull punches, calling this whole narrative "classist bullshit." The prevalent cliché of millennials is that we expect everything to be handed to us, but there are plenty of young people who never expected to do well or to have any help from their teachers, their government, or any support network that they were supposed to be able to count on—let alone feel entitled to anything.

"Most working-class and poor young people in this country are just constantly bumping up against institutions that are failing them and against increasingly fragile families and an unstable job market. It's just ridiculously low wages, an economy that they have no hope of climbing out of, and it's really not about entitlement or expectations at all," Aronowitz said. "They have such low expectations of themselves and their families in the first place. And that's the real tragedy."

Some, she said, don't even know the term *millennial*. Even

if they're in the supermarket and incidentally see, let's say, the *Time* magazine cover about millennials, they wouldn't apply it to themselves. They might not even be on the Internet in the way we think of millennials as being: They have phones, but they don't have unlimited Internet access and may not have any Internet at home. No Twitter. No Instagram. Or, at least, no prioritizing of these apps in their daily lives.

Giving a name to 80 million people in a generation has a trickle-down effect to policy, and if you're not talking about the millions of millennials who are in poverty, then they are ignored in a tangible, political way. When we talk about eliminating student debt or making the housing market better for young people, we're thinking of upper- to middle-class millennials, not about the problems of all sorts of millennials.

Reporting on millennials who aren't white or middle class never uses the word *millennial.* The multitudes of Asian New York City nail salon workers profiled in the viral 2015 *New York Times* piece "The Price of Nice Nails"? Millennials. Homeless queer youth? Millennials. Black men incarcerated at higher rates? Millennials. Sandra Bland when she died in police custody as the result of a traffic stop? A 28-year-old millennial.

Millennials largely have low-wage jobs in retail or the service industry, according to Aronowitz's reporting. They are still going to college, but increasingly to vocational schools, preprofessional colleges, community colleges, junior colleges, or for-profit colleges. Aronowitz said the average age a woman has a child now in the United States is 25—"squarely millennials." (Yet the millennial women portrayed in the media are the upper- to middle-class ones waiting to have a baby because they're too "self-centered" and "career-driven.") The 2016 Census reported that one-third of millennials are living in multigenerational households with either their parents or the millennial's kids, or both. They live with their parents to save money, help out, and secure child care.

Grace Esparza, a 25-year-old Latina living in Chicago, is a millennial living in a multigenerational household. She moved to Chicago from Kirkland, Illinois, to attend Loyola University on a scholarship, and she took her mother and two sisters with her. Esparza said in a Skype interview with me that she couldn't have afforded to not live at home and her mother still needed her help with her younger siblings. They got an apartment together, one bus ride away from campus because as a student, Grace could get a free bus pass. Her family's food stamps also eased some of her college food costs. She's taking advantage of every opportunity to save money. "I've been poor my whole life, so I was really really good at that," she said.

When I put a call out on Twitter for this book, looking for millennials of color doing unpaid internships, it wasn't middle- to upper-class kids who emailed me. It was mostly women like Grace, who fit Aronowitz's profile of the forgotten lower-income millennial. Midway through our Skype conversation, Grace had to check if we got disconnected because her Internet bill wasn't paid that month. These types of financial problems don't mesh with *Time* writer Joel Stein's portrait of a whining twenty-something who wants endless vacation days at work and to eat overpriced avocado toast everyday. The middle class is millennial. The poor are apparently just a permanent underclass. That needs to change.

TAKEAWAYS

- Take everything you hear about millennials or any other generation with a grain of salt (yes, even the stuff in this book). The generalizations often don't consider the full diversity of these populations.

- Be open about your own money foibles with your friends your own age and with the older and younger people you know. Tell them the errors of your (and society's) ways. They are learning from our mistakes—and we can learn new money techniques from them too.

- Stop ragging on millennials as some mysterious terrible monolith. We're sorry we're not spending as much on cereal or diamonds or whatever, the way previous generations did. We inherited a shitshow.

6

#FREELANCELYFE

In 2013, I moved to LA from New York. I was able to keep my full-time reporting job at the *Daily Dot* by working remotely and from home. After a few months in LA, I quit the *Daily Dot* and took a local job blogging for an Internet news recap show. I sometimes appeared on the show, which had some notoriety in the YouTube community. My following on social media grew again, but our boss was an unreliable weirdo who eventually fired me for, I assume, not . . . blogging enough? I went back to freelance writing for magazines and other publications like I had been in NYC, but it wasn't good money. I needed another income stream. Fast.

That's when I decided to nude-model. I thought maybe I could eventually become a Suicide Girl. Suicide Girls, named after a line in a Chuck Palahniuk book called *Survivor*, are models that have piercings or tattoos, or both, as I did at the time. I made an account on ModelMayhem, the Craigslist of modeling. The photographers are equal parts legit and creeps. Like in the actual modeling industry, I imagine, it's hard to discern who is what.

I modeled three times. Nothing untoward ever happened to me. All three male photographers I worked with were respectful, but I had no prior knowledge of how this kind of work was supposed to go and could have easily been walking right into my death. Obviously, the photos are out there and they circulate every so often. I'm not shy about my body. Luckily, I also work in an industry where my having gotten paid for nude modeling isn't a deal breaker. In fact, I modeled nude again in 2017 for an anti-slut shaming campaign for which I did not get paid but which *was* a good cause. (This is what I said to convince my manager to let me do it.)

I didn't know what to charge for nude modeling (advice sites vary from $15 to $60 an hour), and I took way less than I should have (around $10 an hour). But with that and You-Tube, it filled the short gap between my other jobs. I also didn't really think about this decision that hard. Maybe I should have. If you want to do something similar, I'd do more research than I did. Are these photographers reputable? What's the right rate to charge? Should I let someone I trust know where I'm going in case shit goes down? (Yes, absolutely. And give a time you're expected to be done so if you're not picking up your phone by then, they can call 911.) Make sure you know you're like me and you won't be bothered by the photos later, or that modeling won't come back to bite you in the ass (pun intended) job-wise or family-wise. (Like my manager, my parents have given up at this point.)

Right as I was getting into this modeling thing, a man who worked at Nickelodeon and had been a fan of my *100 Interviews* blog reached out and asked if I wanted to work in a writers' room for a children's sketch comedy show. My 2011 post on *100 Interviews* looking for people to hire me had paid off three years later.

Right after this writer's room ended, someone else who had enjoyed *100 Interviews* emailed me to ask if I'd want to do a six-week residency at Buzzfeed Video. I parlayed that into a full-time writing gig in its video department. My salary was $55,000 a year. My BFF Allison and I already had our own comedy YouTube channel, *Just Between Us*, with a small 5,000-fan subscriber base. I'd met Allison soon after I moved to Los Angeles at a stand-up-comedy open mic.

One day, one of the video producers at Buzzfeed was looking for two female best friends to star in a video they called *If Girl Best Friends Acted Like Guy Best Friends*. He asked me if I'd want to be in it and if I had a real-life best friend. BOY, DID I! Allison and I starred in that video together, and from there, she was also hired at Buzzfeed.

The downside to a job like this is that when you create for a media company, often that company owns all your work. When you leave, you have to start from scratch. But by the time we were ready to leave Buzzfeed in 2015, we'd grown our own channel and actually had intellectual property that we owned with our side project, *Just Between Us* (JBU).

After we quit, I got by on the JBU channel and some sporadic acting and writing work. The channel got a few branded deals where we shilled for companies for anywhere from $1,000 to $5,000, income that Allison and I split. (Usually this went directly to my rent and bills.) Our agent took 10 percent. These opportunities were few and far between. I still had no savings or a cushion in case of an emergency. I started driving for Postmates, a food delivery app. To get a job there, I showed up at a very long and boring training session in downtown LA. I was one of probably fifty people there, all desperate to participate in the gig economy for peanuts on the dollar. I felt faceless and worthless. But it was lucky I even had the option of doing this kind of job.

Many, many job-seekers feel the same way. The gig economy has been thriving over the past ten years. In 2016, the Pew Research Center reported that almost 25 percent of Americans made money on a digital earning platform, like Airbnb or Lyft, that year. Thirty-seven percent said that like me, it filled gaps in their employment, 17 percent said it was because of a lack of other available jobs, and 15 percent said they needed the flexible schedule because of other obligations.

Though taking gigs is not new, the phenomenon has exploded with the introduction of apps. The percentage of Americans in the gig economy is "expected to be 43% by the year 2020," Intuit CEO Brad Smith said in May 2017.

The gig economy boom can be linked to the normalization of the "side hustle." (Warning: Googling "side hustle" leads to some truly disturbing auto-fills like "illegal side hustle" and "side hustles for nurses or teachers." The former is disturbing for obvious reasons and the latter because those are jobs that should pay enough.)

Past generations may have taken on extra work to save for a specific expense or splurge, but Bankrate reported in 2017 that 61 percent of current young people say they earn and use their side hustle money every week. Meanwhile, the Freelancers Union and Upwork predicted all kinds of free-lancers will make up a majority of the U.S. workforce within a decade. This is very different from yesteryear's forty years at one company and then a gold watch and a pension.

While these gigs are lifesavers for many people or even just passion projects, I am skeptical of the increased nor-malization of needing to overwork yourself in order to keep afloat, a necessity born out of lower wages and increased health care and housing costs. One nightmare viral post that circulated last year showed a ride-sharing app congratulating a new mom who drove into her ninth month of pregnancy. Why does this need to happen in a First World country? Why do our homes need to become hotels? Why do our cars need to become taxis? Why do we need to be working past work hours? How could I be a full-time reporter or content creator at a media company, working sometimes more than forty hours a week, and still need another job? (I mean, I know how, but you get it.)

In 2015, I channeled my frustrations into an article for *Fusion*, "Get Rich or Die Vlogging: The Sad Economics of Internet Fame." In the piece, I revealed that the videos I was creating were costing me more money than I was making. I described scenes of me crying as I searched for quarters in my car and other very unglamorous aspects of my life that surprised a lot of my followers.

But here's how it works. YouTubers are paid through the

ads that play before their videos, facilitated through Google AdSense. Advertisers can choose what sort of content they want their ads to appear on. YouTube is allowing advertisers to opt out of LGBTQ content, which is basically my bread and butter. Even before these new advertising rules, the Adsense checks were notoriously small. One friend said she makes 89 cents per video. Right now, in 2018, Allison and I have 750,000 YouTube subscribers, and we make about $4,000 a month, which we split. (This again, thankfully, covers my rent and bills, but *only* my rent and bills.) Back when we started, it was *much* less.

In my *Fusion* article, I wrote about my friend Brittany Ashley, who was one of the most popular actresses on Buzzfeed's multimillion subscriber channels but who also worked as a waitress to survive. "Customers had approached her at work before, starstruck but confused," I wrote in the article, "*'Why would someone with 90,000 Instagram followers be serving brunch?'* Simple: because Ashley needed the money. And yet, she said, 'as I started having more visibility on the internet, I had to scale back on serving people.' Her wallet took the hit, and so did her pride. 'My coworkers would tell me a table of kids was freaking out [about seeing me] and I'm like, 'What? Am I going to go say hi and take a picture in my work uniform?'"

This was the case for me and Postmates as well. Postmates workers are given a time limit during which they have to deliver their order (usually thirty minutes). Once I was stopped for photos and almost missed my delivery window, which would have meant I wasn't going to get paid. But how could I explain to an excited fan on the street that I was in a rush?

As I say in the piece, "Many famous social media stars are too visible to have 'real' jobs, but too broke not to."

This was the cost of my risky decision to leave Buzzfeed (a steady paycheck) for the great unknown.

A month after we quit, Allison and I got a big break: We sold a half-hour comedy to MTV, and our careers kept advancing. But the sale was for very little money, and the show didn't get past the pilot. (Sometimes a network will shoot thirty pilots and only send three to series. It's a crapshoot.)

But after that sale, we were able to then sell a TV show to FX in 2016, and this one went for a significantly larger amount of money: $50,000 aka the money that changed my life. It was the most money I'd ever seen. I wasn't even sure my bank account could handle it, so I called and asked. I would not have been able to continue to survive in LA if this script sale had not happened. I used it on a couple of trips to see my family in Florida; to completely pay off a car loan, my dental debt, and two of my smaller student loans; and to pay down one way-overused credit card. I also put some into a retirement fund.

But that FX show didn't get made either. (You still get paid for shows that don't go. This whole industry is super weird.) After that, we sold YET ANOTHER television show, this time to YouTube Red, YouTube's subscription service, though for way less money than the FX show. It did not get made either. (Don't feel badly for us. *You're the Worst* creator Stephen Falk once told us that he sold nine shows before he got anything on the air.) That smaller amount went into retirement, savings, and toward another maxed-out credit card.

Allison and I have made most of our money selling these

unaired shows. I also get paid to host my podcast, *Bad with Money*, through ads placed on the show (similar to Google AdSense income) which I split fifty-fifty with the podcast network.

Currently, I make much of my monthly income through brand deals, which include posts on Instagram and Twitter and videos on YouTube. A brand like Google Home or HelloFresh or the sex toy company Adam & Eve will pay me a fee to advertise for their company or product on my accounts (because they know I can reach a wide audience). But brand deals come infrequently, and the pricing is all over the place. Fans also HATE brand deals, and if I post too often, they feel they're being inundated with ads and may unsubscribe or unfollow. I have to maintain a balance—and often turn down lucrative deals that might alienate my fans.

I also work various other freelance writing and acting gigs that cut me small checks to keep the Gaby machine going. (The Gaby machine is fed by cheese.) Payments vary: Some publications pay as much as $2 a word, and others are $50 for the whole article. In 2018, I appeared on a sitcom that was eventually sold to Starz. I get speaking fees for talks about LGBTQ issues or personal finance or other topics I'm an "expert" on, so, for example, if I spend five days as a guest at Autostraddle Camp, an annual retreat for queer women, the organization might pay me $500 for my time. All these little things come together to make me a yearly salary that is then taxed A LOT. (We'll get to that in Chapter 10, "The Tax (Wo)Man.")

Having bits and pieces of jobs that make up your income is common these days. Almost everyone I know is in that situation. Some have full-time jobs and do their side hustle, and others make all the hustles into one "job." Friends of mine babysit because the hours are flexible and because you can sometimes get creative work done while the kid is napping. Other friends drive Lyft or Uber (like my dad does). Or they work for Postmates or sign up for other apps like Fiverr, TaskRabbit, or Handy. My friend Ariana reads people's tarot cards out of her home. She also delivers pizzas. (Apparently pizza places are always looking for drivers, and one perk is if the person doesn't answer the door in time, you as the driver get to keep the pizza, at least according to Ariana's Instagram.) My friend Emily teaches children's yoga.

My sister, on top of her porn marketing job, has been getting really good at selling electronics on eBay. In the last month, she's sold an Alexa, which I got for free at a YouTube convention and never used (paranoia!), and a pair of Beats by Dre headphones that I also never used. These things netted us $300. (I split it with her to compensate her for her time.)

Jobs today are scattershot. Many of us have work that is never stable, guaranteed, or predictable. It is hard to explain to my grandmother how or why I make money. ("People pay you to post? On the Internet? Why? What do you do during the day?")

I've been able to put together some savings and a small retirement fund from what I've made in the past couple years, but a lot of my recent income went to fixing ten years of irresponsibility—paying back loans and various forms of debt. I'm not out of the woods yet, and because of the way my industry goes, my status can change at any minute. But that lump sum from FX when I was 28 years old allowed me to start filling in the hole and putting a little money away. And sometimes I still end up in an unexpected money bind that requires a quick eBay or freelance writing hustle.

You don't have to work for an app, although those jobs are the easiest/most common to secure. I worry the market is oversaturated, and there might not be enough work for how many people want to work for apps now. But there are also more apps! One graphic designer friend makes flyers for clients on Fiverr, an app that lets people pay five bucks (or more) for any number of services. If you can provide something someone might wanna throw five bucks at, sign up. (There are also similar apps like the ones I mentioned before, TaskRabbit and Handy.)

If you want to freelance write or draw, make sure you look over every contract you're given and ask a lot of questions. I constantly worried about seeming annoying, but it's better to be annoying and protect yourself than to let someone take advantage of you. (If you can have a lawyer or lawyer friend or friend in law school look it over for you, even better.) Make sure there's a date in writing by which they have to pay you. (No one ever wants to pay you on time.)

Other side hustles can come from your own creativity. A friend named Sam makes limited-run T-shirts based on current events. For instance, if Beyoncé does something amazing, Sam will have a shirt ready for sale in a few hours to capitalize on the trend. They sell out super fast.

The key to a fruitful side hustle is to be passionate about the subject matter. My girlfriend and I just started selling custom-designed LGBTQ-themed hand towels online because we can make a little profit. (And I love danger. Spontaneously starting a small business with a romantic partner?

Let's do this.) We care about the LGBTQ community. Sam cares about Beyoncé. My other friend loves graphic design. My dad enjoys driving and meeting new people. Can every job be 100 percent enjoyable? Sadly, no. Most aren't. But it helps if what you're doing in your free time makes you money and fulfills something you're maybe not getting in your day job. Or, like in my case, you need multiple income streams to keep you afloat.

I always keep the idea of the side hustle in my back pocket. If a brand takes a full year to cut me a check (which happens), I sell old action figures online to keep myself in the black. If our monthly YouTube ads payment is low, I bring clothes over to Buffalo Exchange so I don't overdraw my account. My girlfriend and my towel idea came from a particularly bad crying session where I was running low on cash and waiting for too many unpredictable freelance payments. The gig economy lives on.

HOW TO APPLY FOR UNEMPLOYMENT

Just in case your side hustle isn't cutting it, each state has a different process for unemployment application, but it's worth doing if you've been fired from your job or otherwise qualify. After you're approved, it usually takes two to three weeks to start receiving checks to tide you over. You can apply on the website for your state's unemployment services or by calling its offices, mailing in a form, or going to the office in person. (Talking to a real person? Awful. Just kidding, just kidding.)

When I applied for unemployment, it was in California,

and I did it by printing out and mailing in the forms. I'm not sure why. Maybe I thought it was more official. Either way, I ended up being denied because it was determined I'd technically quit, but the application for unemployment was pretty basic. (You have to give the reason you no longer have a job and prove you were let go through no fault of your own. I did not prove that. That's on me.)

They'll ask for information like your name, Social Security number, and the name, address, and phone number of your former employer. Just like with a W-2 form, you can ask that taxes be taken out in the paycheck itself. (I opted for this on my denied application; I didn't want to pay taxes in a lump sum later.)

Then you get a log-in and file each week for your payment. You won't get paid unless you file. You can get direct deposit too, which is very convenient. You can also check on your online account to see how much compensation you have left.

There's absolutely no shame in getting unemployment. In fact, I'll yell at you if you don't. Get all the help offered. Don't feel badly about it.

TAKEAWAYS

- The upshot of the gig economy is that it's easy to find "side hustles" to make ends meet, but it can feel very unstable and stressful juggling all those different jobs. Try to create a schedule for yourself that replicates a working week schedule and solidify a reasonable number of working to not-working hours.

- Be prepared to go through several hustles before you find one that works out.

- Even when someone seems successful, don't make assumptions about how much that person is making. It may be a lot; it may not be. You don't know their expenses or history with money. Income does not necessarily equal wealth.

- Let's all be more transparent about how we get our money! We have to make it, so we should be honest about where it's coming from. Sharing this information with friends helps us not feel so isolated and might provide leads for future income.

- Ain't no shame in the applying-for-unemployment game!

CHEYANNE'S STEPS FOR SELLING STUFF ON EBAY

My little sister has recently become an eBay savant. She highly recommends it because it has the ideal money-to-effort ratio. Here are her steps for selling your stuff online. (I've also had some of my own success on Craigslist where, not to brag, I sold both a microwave and a space heater in less than a day.)

1. Look into what price the other people on the site or stores are charging for the same item to understand what's reasonable to ask. "Some people price too high and then don't sell things," Cheyanne said. "I found if you have a good middle ground on the price, you'll still get a good amount for your stuff and it won't take forever to sell."

2. Upload your own pictures of your products rather than using ones from online. Buyers are more likely to view and purchase the product.

3. You can have people bid on an item, or you can set it up so they can "buy it now" at a set price, so if someone really wants it, they can buy it without having to bid and you get paid without having to wait for bidding to end. You might lose out on higher bids, but you also might get paid quicker.

4. Once the product is sold, eBay sends an invoice to the buyer and sends the seller an email to purchase the postage online. (It's a nice add-on to include postage in the buyer's final price.) You print the postage, send the package at the post office, and get a tracking number.

5. Usually the money comes within a week or so. Cheyanne said she uses the online money transfer service PayPal and then moves it to her bank account. She's made $450 on three items in just two months so far. Not too shabby for not needing to leave the couch.

7

BIPOLAR II: THE SEQUEL

The first couple of times I was given the diagnosis bipolar II, I ignored it. I didn't tell my parents or my friends. I never followed up. I just pretended I hadn't heard it.

Bipolar is a mood disorder with two main mood swings: depression (down) and mania (up). Depression alone is a bit more common and, in my experience, easier for the average person to understand. But depression does not just mean sad. When I'm depressed, I'm in physical pain. Mania, or hypomania, is harder to grasp. Mania can be euphoric (nothing can stop you; you're the best) or depressive (mean, desperate). Either way, I stop thinking. I lose control.

Bipolar disorder is episodic. A person with bipolar can seem very stable for a long time and then suddenly go off the rails. Without medication, this is what happens to me.

The only time I'd privately hinted to another person that

I might be bipolar was in a conversation with my mom when I was visiting from New York in 2011. We were sitting at the kitchen table, and I told her a therapist suggested the condition might apply to me. Her response was something about how all the women on her side of the family have "mood swings." I'd said, "Yes, bipolar disorder is genetic. It would make sense if we were all bipolar." She'd shrugged it off. A specific diagnosis didn't seem important to her; it was just a family curse. I never followed up on my therapist's opinion.

I'd always seen a talk therapist—either cheaply by going to a student therapist for a discount (twenty-five bucks a session) or, when I made some more money, going to a "real therapist." Changing therapists all the time depending on what you can afford isn't the best way to get consistent care. I told friends that I was in talk therapy. Because this was NYC, everyone who could afford it was in talk therapy, and those who couldn't wished they were. But seeing a psychiatrist was a different story. Medication meant something was *really* wrong with you. (Ironically, recreationally taking Adderall or Xanax was much more accepted.)

The only public hint I gave to being bipolar was in 2012 when I wrote "What It's Like to Be Manic," an article for *Thought Catalog*. I never specified if it was fiction or nonfiction; the site trafficked in both. Even in that article, I purposefully didn't use the word *bipolar* because I was too scared of the scarlet B of the stigma. I was—and am—terrified of being written off as "crazy."

For someone who makes a living being transparent about her life on the Internet, I've left out a big chunk of my story. So I'll come clean here: I'm bipolar. For as long as it has taken me to open up about my disorder, it has taken me even longer to connect the dots between my mental health and my finances. Here's a snippet of the piece I wrote in 2012, explaining my brain on mania:

> *Then it's three hours later and I've learned a few phrases in Mandarin and looked up good science graduate programs and bought a book on eBay about musical writing and none of this is actually useful. I've just made myself sick with expectations and self-imposed "musts."*

This includes spending money I didn't have on whims I didn't need. I told myself all of these impulsive purchases were "deserved." There were specific purchases I *needed* to do my best work—for instance, the book on writing musicals. (I never wrote a musical unless you count my unproduced treatment for the rock opera *What's My Age Again? The Blink 182-sical.* Mark Hoppus, call me.)

The only way I could write my new brilliant novel or my award-winning article idea was if I bought myself a new computer. I'd stay up all night talking myself into filling out graduate school applications for schools in Japan and buying books on Japanese culture.

When I was manic, I wanted to spend all my money because life was a breeze, and who cared about social constructs like money? When I was down, I desperately needed material things to make me feel better. No matter what state I was in, I convinced myself not to look at my finances or try to sort out my bank accounts or plan for the future because it was "too stressful" and I was "too fragile right now."

My first "breakdown" took place in 2008 when I was a sophomore in college. I had become too anxious to eat, and so I was stick thin and shaking constantly. I don't fully remember how that episode ended but all I know is (1) in photos of myself from back then, I am pale and sickly (in one set, I'm on the beach with my friends and my legs look like knobby toothpicks) and (2) I never did anything to fix it. I waited it out and kept working myself to death at my *Globe* job and at school (the newspaper, the honors program, classes). Just like my money troubles, my mental health was a pattern I was staving off instead of treating. I didn't go on meds then because the idea never occurred to me. The anxiety eventually became more manageable, and I convinced myself it was a fluke.

Four years later, in May 2012, I crashed again. This was the second time I'd gone from intense manic work ethic to crushing suicidal depression in the course of one year, but I still didn't understand that my brain chemistry might be to blame.

When it happened in 2012, I'd been riding high—so high, in fact, that although I didn't have any health insurance, I decided to undergo minor surgery to correct a broken blood vessel on my lower lip. It was a purely cosmetic choice. My pink lips had a small red dot on them that had been there for years and caused me no physical pain. I became fixated on it, thinking it made me ugly. (Other people barely noticed it.)

I went to an outpatient surgeon my grandmother recommended who said he could laser the blood vessel's coloration back to pink for a few thousand dollars I didn't have. I put it on my credit card and got the surgery. I honestly do not know what I was thinking. I just got the idea in my head that I *needed* to fix this little dark spot and that once I did, everything in my life would fall into place. I procured a bunch of medical debt for no apparent reason. The crash was coming at me like a shark with the *Jaws* theme song playing behind him.

When my birthday came around in June, I threw myself a massive party at the improv theater where I performed in downtown NYC. The boy I was interested in didn't show up because he was fighting with his girlfriend, so I got super-super-drunk. I ended up going home with two male friends and having a very fun but very ill-advised threesome (ill advised because they were colleagues and I was mixing business and pleasure). I took a too-expensive cab back up to my place in Harlem in the small hours of the morning and promptly passed out.

The next day, I woke up with a massive hangover, and I couldn't stop shaking. (Alcohol can exacerbate mental illness because it's a depressant.) My hangover eventually subsided, but later that night, I was still feeling very crappy. I also had not stopped convulsing, shuddering every so often between waves of nausea. I'd had bad hangovers before, but this was more than that. I was totally unable to eat. The mere thought of food caused the shaking to intensify. I tried to eat some cooked spinach, which I normally love, and I threw it up violently. Something was really wrong.

My sister-in-law drove to Brooklyn from Nyack and picked me up at the apartment of a girl I was casually seeing. She took me back to her and my brother's two-bedroom condo outside the city. I spent the next week in the same smelly

gray pajamas, unable to get off their couch. I could barely
move unless it was to blink. I stared off into nothing, basically
comatose. I couldn't keep food down, but I also couldn't even
get it into my mouth. I'd eat one piece of banana and shake for
an hour. I moaned and cried. My whole body was in physical
pain. I couldn't express what was wrong, and so I didn't talk.
I did not sleep. In the middle of one of the nights I was there,
I lay on the floor of my brother's bedroom, screaming and
begging my brother to call 911 because I was convinced I
was dying. They had a 2-year-old son, by the way. They could
not also handle my grown-lady psychosis. Every second, I
was more and more convinced I was having some kind of pro-
longed heart attack because my chest was in so much pain. I
couldn't take a full breath. I thought I had to die to feel better.

Eventually I became okay enough (or annoying enough)
to be allowed to go back to my apartment in Harlem. I was
embarrassed to have been such a burden on my family. Luckily, I was working for a blog where people sometimes failed
to show up to work due to *cocaine*. My taking some time because of my bad brain chemistry was totally within reason. I
must have gone back to working, but I don't remember it. I
figured this extreme manic-depressive episode was a one-off
(or a two-off, thinking back to 2008).

———

But two days later, I bought . . . wait for it . . . a plane ticket
to Europe.

Yes. You read that right. I spent the remaining money I
had in my bank account, which was maybe $800, on a non-

stop flight to Paris on a boutique airline. I planned to go for two whole weeks. A coworker at *Thought Catalog* lived in Paris, and I thought I could lean on her for a place to stay for at least a couple days. (Had I asked her before booking? Of course not.) I also had a friend who lived and worked in Madrid, and I wanted to visit her. I thought, *The real reason I got sick is I am too stressed out. I deserve a vacation.* I was still panicked constantly, couldn't afford any more time off work, and certainly had no money to pay for accommodations or tourist attractions or food. So too soon after my mental breakdown, I had changed nothing about my lifestyle and was off on an impromptu expensive vacation.

In Europe, I slowly went more insane. I had done no research. I was not aware of the exchange rate, so I used that as an excuse to not understand how much I was spending. I was there by myself, so I visited all the landmarks alone, but it was hard to keep myself busy during the day. I had too much anxiety to talk to anyone, and my one friend in Paris was working because she was a person with an apartment and a boyfriend and, you know, a whole life that wasn't about me. I had not planned this trip at all. At night, to assuage my anxiety, I drank a lot. Then the next morning when I was sightseeing, I would feel sick. One day I took a train to Versailles and realized I had no money to eat while I was there, but it didn't matter because the combination of hangover and anxiety made me throw up on the lawn of the palace. I wrote in my journal for that day, "Do you think Marie Antoinette ever vomited here?"

I don't mean to seem ungrateful about spending time among the beauty of Europe. A highlight was meeting my grandmother's cousin and being able to take photos with him that my grandmother still cherishes. I also rode the train to Brussels, where I had one of the best days of my life. I met a family there that paid for all my food and let me hang out with them—a twelve-person midwestern family of teenagers and middle-aged adults who bought me waffles and chocolate and mussels and pasta and beer. One of the women told me, "We'd hope your parents would do that for one of our kids if the situation was reversed."

I had a great time in Madrid, where I stayed with my friend who lives there. The song "Call Me Maybe" had just come out, and every nightclub we partied at played nothing else. I got too drunk, made out with some dude while a Spanish cover band butchered the Red Hot Chili Peppers' "Dani California," and did not sleep for three days. In terms of money, I may as well have just opened a suitcase of it and let it fly out into the Grand Canyon. I started to put everything on my credit card, which had a $5,000 limit that had already been tested with my unnecessary lip surgery. I wrote this in my journal:

> *So stupid and unanticipated to be in Paris and to be lonely. I often feel alone in New York but not like this. Had that sense again of "Wherever you go, there you are" in that traveling somewhere else doesn't mean you can escape yourself. It's not the city that makes the difference. Not that getting to see and understand the endless, overwhelming world isn't helpful or that I don't appreciate how beautiful everything is and how lucky I am to finally be doing this—since I often feel this weird weight about not being*

able to experience everything that's out there. But at the same time, it'd be better with people. I thought going on this trip would cure my depression or instantly make me a better, more well-rounded person, but that's not the case. It's not traveling; it's human interaction—from the Ozarks to Japan to Canada to wherever you go—it's having other people around to share what you're doing. Someone once wrote on one of my Thought Catalog *articles, "If everyone feels alone, why can't we all just find each other?" I don't know if it's that easy, but I do know now that I have to be okay where I am, before I can be okay anywhere else.*

I was starting to get it, but my behavior was not going to catch up just yet.

I went back to Paris from Madrid for another few days because I was flying out of Charles de Gaulle airport. My last day in Paris, I went to a lesbian bar with a girl I was sort of dating's ex who was also visiting the city (classic queer women triangulation). Leaving the bar, I reached into my purse and realized my wallet had been stolen. I had my passport in my bag, so I could feasibly get home, but I'd lost my credit and debit cards, $80 in cash, and a pair of earrings I'd bought in New Orleans that had sentimental value. We retraced my steps and found nothing.

My friend and I went to the local police station to report my wallet stolen, but they were no help. (I imagine the French police blowing cigarette smoke in my face, but I know that didn't happen.) I filed a report, but it was useless. I had to get on a plane that next morning. My friend gave me some money for a couple of taxis. I went back to my Airbnb, packed my things, and headed straight to the airport. I didn't want to spend another minute on the Paris streets, which now seemed like a sobering sinkhole for money.

I got on my early-morning flight and did not have money for food the whole trip. I was starving. When I got to JFK, I realized I didn't have my MetroCard to get home. I called my ex-boyfriend, the comedy writer Josh Gondelman, an actual angel on planet Earth, and begged him to come pick me up at the airport in his car. On the way home, he was way too gentle with me but chided me a little on my choices. (He should have been way madder than he was. We'd broken up in April, and here he was picking me up from the airport after I'd been reckless.) I went to the bank and got a temporary debit card, and eventually I replaced the things in my wallet—except for the cash and earrings. Emotionally and financially, I was at my lowest.

I went back to my day job and took on more hours. Eventually I left to take a higher-paying full-time job with much-needed benefits at the *Daily Dot*, a newsy site where I was working as a reporter instead of as a blogger, thus finally putting my expensive journalism degree to use. DD paid more, and I desperately needed a higher salary.

I still had credit card debt from my mania, but I never thought about it. I figured it was a problem that future-me could deal with. I was convinced I was special and was going to succeed so wildly at this young age that the debt didn't matter. It was the era of Donald Glover and Lady Gaga after all. I was meant to make millions by the time I was 25. (To be "25 sitting on 25 mil," as Drake put it.)

On the rare occasions that I logged into Bank of America

online, I would peek at the number in my checking account and then close it quickly like it was an ancient cursed book. I overdrafted constantly. Every time I ran out of money, my mom would, behind my dad's back, put fifty bucks into my account to cover the $30 overdraft fee and give me twenty bucks to play with. (Love, but also enabling!) The boat kept filling with water, and I kept trying to drain it with a thimble.

I talked about this with NO ONE. I figured everyone I knew was doing the same thing, racking up credit card debt and praying for a light at the end of the tunnel.

My mental health spiraled downward. My shakiness and anxiety hadn't fully subsided since the summer, and so I decided it couldn't hurt to look into medical help beyond talk therapy. In winter 2012, I started seeing a very cheap, pay-as-you-can psychiatrist who prescribed me Klonopin and Celexa. The combo made me fall asleep in the shower and bruise my head. On this medication cocktail, I was exhausted. I slept for days. I missed work. My roommate called my parents. I'd been acting like a zombie and was speaking incoherently.

One night, I woke up in a haze with my dad standing over me. He'd flown from South Florida to bring me home. I didn't want to go. I had comedy shows to perform. I had to try to go back to work. My dad did not give me a choice about it. The next day, he essentially forced me onto a plane to Fort Lauderdale for my own good.

I spent the next month in a parentally devised "rehab." I went off the meds I'd been on. I saw and spoke to almost no one other than my family members, my dad's AA friends, and a yoga instructor. Every morning, my mom woke me up at

6:00 a.m. and dragged me to kundalini yoga (the deep breath-
ing kind). She forced me to eat bananas and cereal while I
shook violently. At lunchtime, she forced me to eat a small
sandwich. In the evenings, I'd go with my dad to AA, or we'd
watch a movie and I'd go to bed early. I did not drink coffee
or soda. I did not drink alcohol. I cried all the time. I slowly
got better.

But I was furious. I was desperate to get back to NYC
where I was still paying the $800 rent on my bedroom in
Harlem. I wasn't spending anything in Florida, but I also
hated the idea of my room sitting empty while I paid for it.
It took a month in Florida for me to regain my strength, and
I convinced my parents to let me go back to the city to attend a fancy dinner party I'd been looking forward to. My
priorities were still the same as they'd ever been. I decided
I couldn't afford new meds, but that it was fine. I was better
now. A year later, I moved to LA. My job provided health insurance, and since I was stressed about the move, I went back
on meds: Zoloft and Klonopin. I thought I was so responsible.
I thought everything was stable.

So when I had another breakdown in 2016 and a psychiatrist in LA asked if I'd ever been diagnosed with bipolar II, I
said yes. I had been. Multiple times.

If I was going to really fix my financial troubles, then
I had to admit there were other things at play beyond irresponsibility and youthful ignorance. I could learn about
taxes and individual retirement accounts, and I could work
really hard to get out of debt, but in the end, I was always
one mental lapse away from destroying my credit score. The
meds for depression weren't fixing the real problem. Eight

years after my first breakdown, I finally started on Lamictal specifically for bipolar disorder, and gradually I got a handle on my brain.

———

I'm not saying medication is the answer for everyone. I'm not a doctor, and I'm not you. Also, my meds are now covered by insurance. My therapist costs me $125 a session and my psychiatrist costs me $225 every two months, but it's money I have now and I'm willing to spend on myself. I know not everyone is in that position. But even more than the meds and doctors, what saved me from financial ruin was realizing that there were other psychological factors that contributed to my overspending.

Julie Fast, a writer, educator, and expert on bipolar disorder, had a long road to diagnosis too. In 1995, she was 31 years old when she was told she had bipolar II, although she said her symptoms started when she was 15. Like me, it took her a while to get to the bottom of why she was so impulsive with spending. Fast was interviewed in a 2013 Reuters article, "When Bipolar Disorder Leads to Extreme Shopping." I found it when I was looking for information on how my disorder affected my spending.

The impulsivity of mania is aided and abetted by shopping apps. People don't even see the cash in their paycheck before it's swiped into Ubers and Amazon Prime. In a 2016 *Vice* article, "Your Mental Health Is Making You Poor," Hazel Sheffield wrote of people with mental illness that "80 percent said they found internet shopping a trigger for spending."

I definitely needed to cut down on my Amazon spending. (Learn more about this in Chapter 9, "A Fad Diet for Your Wallet.") The whole "now anyone can indulge any passing whim with the click of a button!" thing hasn't exactly been ideal for me. I know that I should also delete Postmates, although as a former employee for that company (when I first moved to LA), I do like supporting the People of the Gig Economy. But both Amazon and Postmates make it easy for me to just order what I need when it'd be just as easy, cheaper, and more ethical to pop over to the local grocery store. Without access to online shopping, I can't just drop $50 on a new jacket because I feel sad. I'd be forced to find another way to correct my mood.

When you're feeling crappy, "comfort spending" lifts your spirits, and when you're flying high, you can experience what's called "manic spending." An example of manic spending is when I feel I worked hard at something and therefore deserve new sneakers immediately. Comfort spending is when I'm sad from working too hard and need new sneakers to feel better. Even if you don't have bipolar disorder, you might be buying material things to fill the emptiness inside.

In her article, Sheffield describes a man who says he was feeling low and flew himself to Paris. (Sound familiar?!)

Here are some things I try to do instead of spending money when I'm sad:

Shower (HUGE! BEST CHOICE!).
Go for a walk or run.
Look at Instagram videos of bunnies.
Become too immersed in bunny culture.
Wonder if I should get a bunny.

Don't. (Close call!)

Circle back to that shower idea.

Drink a juice.

Look at old pictures of my sister and me when we had bad haircuts.

Read a book.

Organize a drawer (Whoa! I have so many highlighters! Amazing!).

Follow another bunny account.

———

Other mental disorders affect spending too. Sheffield writes that post-traumatic stress disorder (PTSD) may lead to nihilistic thoughts like "Who cares how much money I spend?" Depression can lead to spending a lot on gifts for friends because of the fear they don't actually like you. Anxiety can cause you to buy twenty-five different types of bug spray before a camping trip because what if twenty-four out of the twenty-five don't work? (You get the picture.)

Avoiding this reckless spending requires getting out ahead of yourself. Julie Fast said she has to be prepared for the trade-off of being briefly high-flying and then spending the next six months cleaning up a mess. Sometimes she goes cash only, getting rid of all her credit cards.

As an experiment, Fast took out $100 in $1 bills and spent a day seeing how much money she spent by paying in $1 bills. She realized her frappe was $5 and her lunch was $30. "It changed my life to see the cash," she said. Even now, if she feels manic, she'll freeze her credit cards, delete apps like Uber and Amazon, and deal only in cash until her impulsivity passes. She recommends taking your credit card information off auto-fill on your computer so you aren't able to buy anything with one click. "Make it so you have to enter your card each time," she said. Stopping to think for even that long could prevent a purchase. If your parent or loved one has a college fund or retirement fund, don't put the bipolar person's name on them or give them access, Fast said. Don't feel badly about this. Be your own stopgap.

Many websites suggest getting a "bipolar buddy" who can check in about your spending if you seem to be acting erratically. When I start talking about redecorating my whole apartment, Allison has already taken on the mantle of telling me no. But maybe it needs to be done in a more official capacity. You can also get out in front of yourself by telling the bank to alert your partner or a friend if they see any unusually large payments. (I never knew this was an option.)

"Manic spending is no different than the hyper-sexuality or anything that comes with mania," Fast said on my podcast. "No frontal lobe. No ability to say I can't afford that. All of that is gone." Mania affects me in other ways too: it makes me super social and highly flirtatious. It scatters my thoughts so I stop and start a million projects (I once wrote sixty pages of a feature film in three days without sleeping). I feel more inclined to drink or do drugs. I can be very fun.

But my definition of fun had to change. I function better when I've had enough sleep, food, and time to myself. I'm safer and less inclined to kamikaze my relationships. I actually finish projects I'm working on. I don't spend the next few days feeling sick.

Yet despite all its debilitating effects, mental illness is romanticized. Ernest Hemingway would starve himself, drink a ton of whiskey, and get inspiration from the paintings at the Louvre. How about the numerous biographies I've read on the manic-depressive artist Vincent van Gogh, who could see the vibrant colors of his work only because of his illness? Could it be that my best work is when I'm sick? (This myth is brilliantly destroyed by comedian Hannah Gadsby in her comedy special "Nanette." Please watch it.) When I relayed this misinformed theory of mine to Fast, she immediately called me on my bullshit: *And how did their lives end? They killed themselves.*

I'll sleep when I'm dead, I thought proudly, not realizing I was probably bringing that day closer.

Money and mental health are tied up in a chicken-and-egg situation. People with severe mental illness are more susceptible to job loss, debt, homelessness, and money mismanagement. And those problems can also lead to poor mental health and keep you from getting treatment. ("It me," as the kids say.)

The Money and Mental Health Policy Institute, which (unsurprisingly) explores the connection between money and mental health, says people in bad financial situations are twice as likely to develop major depression.

"We can work when we're depressed; it just doesn't feel good," Fast said, adding that she purposefully taught herself to work through her ups and her downs. "The secret I learned and that I teach everybody is if you wait for motivation to show up when you're depressed, it's never going to show up. If you wait to feel good about what you're doing when you're depressed, it will never happen. But if you just put one foot forward and you put yourself out there and you do the work while you're in pain, while you think you can't work, would you believe that you cannot tell the difference between the work you do when you're depressed and what you do when you're stable? Depression doesn't affect our ability to work; it affects our ability to *believe* we can work. It's a really big difference."

Sometimes during bouts of depression, I can't stand up because of the physical pain in my chest and back. I have also struggled with changing meds and adjusting to new dosages that led to days of nausea and the inability to gather my hazy thoughts. How could I work under those conditions? But, like Fast, I had to, so I just did. I still have these blue periods with days of painful sobbing. I still overspend on manic impulse buys and have to constantly stop myself from getting a puppy on a whim. But I'm aware of it, and I am being treated for it with medication and lots of therapy.

The comedian Sara Schaefer, who speaks openly about her mental health in her stand-up, told me in a 2016 episode of my podcast that she had $65,000 of credit card debt because she used money as a way to regulate her depression. "I would get depressed, and I would shop alone. I still like shopping alone. I don't like people being there, because I don't like judgment," she said. When you're depressed and you feel like you can't control anything, making a purchase is something you can control.

Starting in childhood, whenever something bad happened,

Schaefer said her parents would buy her a Pound Puppy (a stuffed animal from the drugstore). She made a "dangerous connection" between spending money and improving your mood. "We'd just started joking that any gift for when you felt bad about anything was just called a Pound Puppy," she said.

"Pound Puppy" is a familiar mollifier, if not a familiar name for it. I'm sure many people in line at a Sephora or Foot Locker right now would tell you the same thing. Buying yourself a little present quiets the sad, even if you don't have a diagnosed mental illness. Spending gets you high. But we can't live our lives surrounded by Pound Puppies. We have to eventually address the barking.

TAKEAWAYS

- Seek out a doctor, a therapist, a support group, a therapy app, an Internet forum, or any other professionals and other people you can talk to specifically about money and your mental health. If you don't know how to find these resources, use the Internet, or ask your primary care physician for recommendations.

- Recruit family and friends to act as your checks and balances. Julie Fast said she has a nephew who will say, "Auntie, you're talking really fast." Her mother can tell she's manic when she texts her late at night. Friends have said, "You're being annoying." The rule is that she can't get mad. She has to take it as a sign she needs help.

- Avoid people who feed your illness. "Friends" who force you to stay out late, drink, or give you a hard time for taking care of your mental health are not your friends.
- Social media can be helpful if used responsibly. If Fast posts on Facebook about how she's feeling (either up or down), she said it's great when people respond with uplifting thoughts or slow-down warnings. But avoid using it to whine too much or to look for validation and enablers. There are always people who are going to be too judgmental or too supportive of bad habits. Filter your posts so only those you trust can see them. (And Facebook's not all that trustworthy, so maybe choose a different avenue, like a personal blog or a private group message.)

8

IMAGINARY MONEY

Here's what I imagined would happen when I got a credit card, having done no research on what happens when you get a credit card:

I walk into the bank. The tellers all stare at me. They smirk. I am prey. I look around the bank, unsure of what to do next. Is someone supposed to come up to you and ask what you want? Do you (as in a restaurant maybe) seat yourself? I see there's a line of people waiting to speak to a teller, but there're also people waiting in chairs to meet with someone in an office. If I wait in the line and then get to the teller and she says, "What? To get a credit card, you have to go talk to a person in an office. Everyone knows that, you moron," then I can never return to this bank. End scene.

When did everyone else learn these things that I imagine are so obvious to the rest of the bank's patrons? Why do I care what the tellers think? I imagine them all going to lunch together and laughing at me. "Can you believe someone reached her age and didn't know who to talk to about getting a credit card?" they'd cackle over pad thai.

Until way late in the game, I had no idea you could get a credit card from anywhere other than a bank. Bank of America (BoA) was the bank my parents used, and that's the only one that gave me any sense of familiarity. When I was kid, the tellers handed me and my sister lollipops for good behavior. I probably had some Pavlovian loyalty to the chain. (Do *all* banks do this?)

When I was a year out of college, I went into a BoA near my apartment in Harlem and got my first credit card. I asked the teller for one credit card, please. I did not know what a credit card was used for other than to get yourself into trouble.

I'm obviously not known for my restraint, but my parents insisted I get a credit card so I could start building a credit score and sign the leases for my own apartments. A terrifying chain of events. At Bank of America, they had me pose for a photo like I was at the Department of Motor Vehicles and then gave me a $5,000 credit limit on a bright red plastic card.

Five thousand dollars. Whoa. I'd never seen $5,000 in any account belonging to me in my entire life.

In the photo, I'm not smiling, and my scarf is wrapped tightly around my neck and over my chin. You can barely see my face. Every time I took the card out of my wallet, it felt like a mirror of my credit-related emotions. Even though I had it, I never looked into what the credit card was for. I never clicked around on the BoA website and checked out my cash rewards or how to get them. I must have known they existed. The card said "cash rewards" right on it. I didn't trust the wording. The whole thing felt like a loaded gun. A trick. Once they got your name and address, they could charge you for all kinds of stuff, and there was nothing you could do. Was I opting into a scam? I slowly started using the card, and though I often got close to maxing it out, I could mostly pay the small minimum and keep the party going.

In August 2017, after having the same credit card for five years, I finally made an appointment at my local Bank of America location, vaguely saying I wanted to "talk about credit cards." I'd never met with anyone at the bank to talk about anything. I allotted an hour for this chat, and I was ready for embarrassment and confusion. But actually, I was in and out in twenty minutes. Here's how it went down:

After a few minutes of relaxing in the waiting chairs (good call on my part!), I was ushered over to a cubicle by a tall bald guy named Tig. Tig showed me that I had $215 in cash rewards that I'd never redeemed. Cash rewards, or cash back, is extra money you get when you use your credit on certain types of expenditures. Each credit card has a different system for rewards (and some have none at all). For example, when I use my card to purchase groceries and gas, a certain percentage of that money is returned to my account as a reward for what I've spent, so I try to be mindful of how I'm using my credit card to maximize the potential for rewards.

At the time I didn't know any of this. Tig helped me redeem my cash rewards ($215! Sitting there!) and set up my account for auto redemption, so that every time the cash rewards hit $25, the money goes directly to my checking account. Tig said this option is useful if I just want the money for immediate use, but less so if I want to save up for something special, like for a gadget. (I see what Tig is into. It's gadgets.)

After my lovely experience at Bank of America, it was hard to swallow the notion that banks are evil empires that control our economy. But the more I was learning, the more that seemed to be the case.

Lisa Servon, author of the book *The Unbanking of America*, which explains why we rely so heavily on banks, says that many people don't have enough money to keep a minimum balance or wait for a check to clear into a bank account. It doesn't help that the minimum balance for free checking is constantly rising; in some cases, it's a few thousand dollars. "More than half of all Americans could not come up with $2,000 in the event of an emergency," she said. If their balance drops below the minimum, they're paying overdraft fees for banking. (PAYING. TO KEEP. YOUR MONEY. IN A BANK. Ugh.) Many low-income people use only cash for these reasons, but there are many vendors out there who don't even take cash or take it only if you spend a certain amount.

Lisa's examples are just some of the practices designed by banks to make money off their customers. Another one is debit resequencing, and it goes like this. You have $100 in your bank account. On Monday morning, the auto-pay you have set up for your phone bill for $75 kicks in. You then go to the grocery store and buy $125 worth of groceries. You also write a check to your landlord for $500. All those charges hit at the same time. What does the bank do? It *could* register the $75 charge first because that would clear. You would then pay two overdraft fees for the other two charges, which would overdraw your checking account.

BUT THAT'S NOT WHAT HAPPENS. Instead, banks use a software program that reorders those charges to put the highest one first. The $500 landlord check hits your account first, making it *three* overdraft fees instead of two. You're fucked.

Nicole Aschoff of *Jacobin* magazine said banks were not always out to get the customer. In the 1970s and 1980s, the US government bent to pressure to deregulate the financial sector. The banks wanted more opportunities to make money and convinced the government this would fix the stagnation of the economy—the declining wages and rising education and health care costs, Aschoff said. The average person hadn't been using credit or loans before. Suddenly they became ubiquitous.

So how can we avoid the big banks and their legalized exploitation? One good alternative to using a bank is joining a credit union. According to MyCreditUnion.gov, a credit union is a nonprofit money exchange set up by an employer, location, family, church, labor union, and many other types of groups. Membership to a credit union can cost anywhere from $5 to $25, and the website allows you to find one near you. In general, a credit union charges you less than a bank will in annual fees. Some reimburse you for ATM fees so you're not losing money because of a lack of available ATMs.

But the big draw is this: 98 million Americans use credit unions because they are run more democratically than banks. (Members get votes on who sits on the union's board of directors, for example.) There are all different kinds of credit unions, including Alliant, Connexus, First Tech, and Golden 1 Credit Union, and each has its own specialty and qualifications. Some are better for businesses, and some are better for students. It depends on what you are looking for, so think about what suits your banking needs and do your research.

Payday lenders are yet another option besides a bank or a credit union, and Servon is a big fan of these. But her love for payday lenders is extremely rare, and her opinion may be somewhat informed by the time she spent working at one in the Bronx while researching her book. The dominant perception is that they take advantage of people. In fact, John Oliver ripped into payday loan centers in a 2014 segment on his show *Last Week Tonight* called "Predatory Lending." Here's a recap of what I learned from it.

A "payday loan" is a loan attained quickly and easily using what's called a payday lender (at a check cashing or payday loan store or online) to cover an "unexpected expense." Also called cash advances, payday loans are meant to be short term. Oliver reported that one in twenty households have taken a payday loan out at some point. It's a $9 billion industry, even as they remain illegal in some states, including Connecticut, Maryland, Vermont, and West Virginia. The problem with payday loans is that they take advantage of vulnerable people who are sometimes unable to pay the loan off on their next "payday" and then reborrow and reborrow, paying larger and larger amounts in interest into oblivion. And unfortunately, as one of the commenters on Oliver's video (which has 9 million views as of fall 2017) said, "Most people who get payday loans probably do not watch John Oliver."

It's tough in any case for this type of argument to persuade low-income people who are, let's say, desperate to pay off a car repair so they can get to their minimum wage job and feed their kids. People who take out these loans end up borrowing money from family, selling plasma, pawning possessions, and taking other desperate measures to pay back the loan that they could have done in the first place *instead* of taking out the loan.

Perhaps. But this point is made more disturbing in a fake commercial during Oliver's segment starring comedian Sarah Silverman in which she tells people thinking of taking out payday loans to do *anything else* to make money: sell sperm (not taking into account the emotional toll of perhaps having children in the world you don't know about or what happens when that kid comes looking for its dad via 23andMe or even if it's possible to donate if you have a disability or low sperm count); or shoplift (been there; not a point of pride for me); or sex work ("pee on people"), a job that is EXTREMELY vilified, can be dangerous, and could cause problems for future employment; or, her final suggestion, "to throw yourself in front of a rich guy's car." (I understand this segment is satire, but all of these suggestions made me feel icky and only highlighted for me why people choose the payday loan route and why poorer people feel misunderstood by liberal media.)

It reminded me of a very sad comical Instagram post by @lineofpepsi that asked "Are you broke?" and then listed options like selling your sperm for $100, eggs for $8,000, bone marrow for $3,000, and then, growing increasingly dark, your corneas for $21,000, your lungs for $295,000, and your heart for $607,000. (The user was joking. Sort of.)

"There's this implicit voice saying if only they acted like me, middle-class white woman with a college education, then they'd make a better decision," Servon said. But in her experience, the check casher was less expensive and more transparent and gave customers more personal service than the bank. Payday lenders might be "more transparent" in Servon's opinion, but that doesn't mean they *are* transparent, especially about the risks and escalating costs. They're an option for people without other options.

It's hard to say who is 100 percent right, and maybe the answer is that no one is. The system's options are all full of consequences. Banks are predatory, payday loan centers are predatory, credit unions aren't open to everyone, burying your money under a tree and hoping it's still there after forty years isn't recommended. Your job is to figure out what feels right to you morally and financially.

HOW TO LEAVE YOUR BANK FOR A COMMUNITY BANK

Fellow queer author Dannielle Owens-Reid wanted to give their money to someone other than a white male executive and/or a big corporation so they took their accounts out of Bank of America and put their money into Broadway Federal Bank, a local Los Angeles black-owned bank. Here's how you can make a similar switch.

1. Make sure the local bank meets the requirements for your life. Dannielle needed a bank that could handle business accounts and found only one local black-owned bank that could, so the decision was essentially made.

2. Be prepared to spend some time at the bank both personally and virtually. Make friends! In terms of personal service, Dannielle said the man in charge of their account at the local bank waives the $12 fee on their business account (which is charged if it falls below $1,000) if they call him and ask. At Bank of America, Dannielle said their business account was charged $16 every time it fell below $2,000, which happened often as it's a new business.

Over the business's first two years, they said, it cost them hundreds of dollars.

3. Know you're buying local. Dannielle's bank operates only in LA, which they love because they are contributing to their own community.

4. Ask about ATMs. Dannielle's new bank doesn't have its own ATMs, but it is connected to STAR ATMs, which are common in Los Angeles. Some places reimburse ATM fees, so ask about that. (This would help me when I drunkenly take out $20. JK. I don't do that anymore.)

5. Beware the skeptics. Lots of people will say what you're doing is "inconvenient." But lots of things that are morally right are inconvenient.

6. Remain resolute. Your old bank may try to get you to stay by telling you about new features you can get on your account or other bargaining chips. Dannielle chose to tell the account manager the real reasons they were leaving, but you can be less confrontational than that. (Ha!)

CREDIT SCORES

Building "good credit" is a task worth taking seriously since it can affect your ability to do so many important human adult things, like rent an apartment, secure a job, buy a car, apply for a good credit card, or take out a loan of any kind.

But what does it mean to have "good credit," and how is it measured? In a basic sense, your credit score is a numerical measurement (ranging from 300 to 850) of how trustworthy you are—more specifically, how likely you are to make timely payments and repayments. The more you do this well, the higher your credit score becomes. For example, student loans build your credit if you're paying them back on time, because it proves to lenders that you're reliable. Late credit card payments will lower your score.

When I received my first significant chunk of income in 2016, I tackled my credit cards and medical debt first, and then moved on to my two smaller student loans (experts recommend that you begin by paying off your credit card debts since they often have higher interest rates than other types of loans).

I still haven't paid off the bigger student loan because it's a flippin' $24,000. I did, however, take this opportunity to check how much interest I was paying on all my loans for the very first time. (Right now, it's 3.8 percent, which seems to be average for undergraduate loans.) Then I looked at the interest payments that had been accruing on my credit card, which was when I learned that the 0 percent interest rate promised to me when I first ordered that credit card had since run out (it was only a year-long perk and I'd had the card for five years). The interest rate was now 22 percent. In

2018, creditcards.com reported that the average interest rate on a credit card was around 16 percent.

So in 2018, I decided to stop using the credit card I had been using for years and order another. I didn't cancel the first one; I just stopped using it as much. My new card currently has 0 percent interest, and after a year, it will have 14 percent, much lower than on my old card.

With all the sign-up bonuses and perks that are offered to you in those mailings from credit card companies, it can be tempting to open up a lot of new ones to get the benefits. But be careful about opening and closing too many credit cards because it can give the appearance of unreliability and lower your credit score.

I didn't know anything about credit cards, but some people make it their livelihood to know *everything* about credit cards. One of them is Brian Kelly, known to the Internet as The Points Guy, who runs a website teaching people how to use credit cards to their advantage.

When I interviewed The Points Guy for this book, his first bit of advice was to check your credit score. (His was too low when he began his journey with credit cards, and he had to work hard to bring it up.) It's possible not to have a credit score at all, but chances are you do have one—and it may even predate you! If your parents ever added you as an additional cardholder on their account, for example, you inherited their credit history, which, if it is good, can help you get a credit card. (Yet another point of disparity between those with wealth history or financially savvy parents and those without. This shit starts before you're even born!)

So where and how do you check your credit score?

You are legally allowed to get your credit score once a year for free without your request having an impact on your score. Your score is affected if you have too many "hard inquiries" like those from lenders or collection agencies because they show unreliability, but your score is not affected by "soft inquiries" like those from the three credit bureaus: Equifax, TransUnion, and Experian. (My credit score is a solid 727, by the way, which is the only bit of money information I LOVE telling people. *Time* magazine said in April 2017 that the average credit score for someone in their late 20s, like me, was 652.)

———

Having a good credit score can be tough. An addict I know checked his credit score for the first time after finally getting sober and found he was screwed. Repairing it required him to get on the phone with multiple financial institutions and government agencies and write many pleading letters. There are credit repair bureaus you can hire to do this, but they might be a waste of money when you can do all the work yourself— that is, only if you have a massive amount of time!

If you find a mistake on your credit report, you can contact the credit bureau and dispute it. Under the Fair Credit Reporting Act, it legally has to investigate the issue, usually within thirty days. Websites like FTC.gov have information about how to correct errors, including a sample dispute letter. Some bureaus accept online disputes; others you have to mail in. (What year is it?) You'll need documentation supporting your claim.

Knowing what exactly determines your credit score can help you figure out how to improve it. FICO, one of the reliable credit score companies that uses past information to predict financial behavior, has an online pie chart outlining the key factors:

1. **PAYMENT HISTORY.** This makes up 35 percent of your score. Paying your credit card bill on time consistently is key because it says a lot about your ability to pay in the future.

2. **AMOUNTS OWED.** This makes up 30 percent. Keep your balances low even if you pay off the minimum. People who constantly reach or exceed their credit limit are seen as a risk.

3. **LENGTH OF CREDIT HISTORY.** This makes up 15 percent. It shows you have a lot of experience in the credit world, which means you're less of a risk. (Is this risk theme coming through?) And credit scores change monthly so scores can go up all the time. Don't lose hope if yours is low.

4. **TYPES OF CREDIT USED.** This makes up 10 percent. Do you have credit cards or loans? If you have credit but not credit cards, this could have a negative impact on your score because you haven't proven to lenders that you can use credit cards responsibly.

5. **NEW CREDIT.** This makes up 10 percent. This reflects how often you open new credit accounts and how often you inquire about your score. This short-

ens the length of each credit history (since they're all so new and do nothing to prove you're good at managing credit long-term, and each time you apply for a new card, a new hard inquiry is done).

It took one person I know *three years* to fully repair his credit. And he had "being a white man" going for him. For marginalized people, especially people of color, credit is even more of an uphill battle. For example, the hilarious black comedian Tiffany Haddish joked on *Late Night with Stephen Colbert* in 2017 that she checked off the "white" box on the Census seven years prior, and "a few days later my credit score went up by 300 points." The audience laughed. The joke works because of the ubiquitous stereotype that black people unfairly have poor credit scores. If Haddish were suddenly white, everyone "knows" her credit score would be better.

I'd be remiss not to mention here that the racism baked into the credit industry stems back hundreds of years. After slavery, many freed slaves were still being jailed for minor crimes, and that continues in the criminal justice system today. After getting out of prison, it was difficult for those same people to get access to loans and credit because they now had criminal records or had to spend too much time behind bars to build good credit.

Later, under redlining, many black and Latinx families were forced to take out home loans from private lenders because banks wouldn't approve them. Credit scoring finds that these loans are seen as "a greater credit risk." A 2017 *North Carolina Law Review* study showed black consumers pay more interest and have cards with lower credit limits. Duke University professor William "Sandy" Darity explained that using a study from Syracuse's Maxwell School of Citizenship and Public Affairs, where researchers had "blacks and whites with comparable credit scores or blacks actually having better credit scores seek home mortgage loans, and they found that the black applicants were more likely to be denied or to be offered loans on considerably worse terms." The process for applying can be anonymous, but the credit card company can see your name (if it's a historically black name) and your address to know the demographics of where you live. "Here's clear and compelling evidence that there was discrimination in the lending process," Darity said.

Credit can be essential to the functioning of many lower-income families, but these same families, lumped together by racist redlining, have a harder time getting approved for credit and a harder time elevating their credit scores enough to get credit cards with which to do the tricks Brian Kelly pulls off. We have to acknowledge this before we begin our journey building credit from scratch.

HOW TO START BUILDING CREDIT FROM SCRATCH

If you want to apply for your first credit card to start building credit, here are some helpful hints:

FIND A COSIGNER. To get a credit card without a credit score, you might need a cosigner—someone with good credit who will sign off on your credit card on your behalf and assume responsibility for your debts if you can't pay them off. Don't not pay them off, or you'll be screwing over someone else too.

GET EMPLOYED. Having a job can make you seem trustworthy enough to get approved for a credit card because it's assumed you'll be able to pay it back every month. (You can get one without a job or if you're a freelancer like I was, but the company or bank will ask for your income so have that information ready.) If you have a solid income, you can be approved without any previous credit. But you can't use your parents' or cosigner's income for this one.

KNOW THYSELF. Figure out what kind of person you are. And I don't just mean are you a Gemini obsessed with true crime documentaries? It's more like: Are you a student? Because there are cards with specific student rewards. (But some of these cards have very high interest rates and fees because who better to scam than students, right?) Do you love to travel? Then you need a travel rewards card. Do you just love cold-hard cash? Cash back, babyyyy. Look at what you actually spend on and where a credit card would help you. (And my fellow Geminis, have you seen the true-crime documentary *The Staircase* because omg, there's no way an *OWL* killed her!!!)

GO SHOPPING. There are also other types of cards: A store credit card is like those Macy's or JCPenney's cards you're offered whenever you're at a department store register. You can use some of these cards only at the corresponding store, but they can really help you build your credit until you can get a "real" card. A secured credit card is one you put "a cash collateral deposit" down on before you can use it. If you put $500 in the account, you can charge up to $500 on the card. (This is good for someone who would have trouble getting a regular credit card but needs one for booking travel or buying online.) Once you have a handle on your credit and can manage a simple credit card, you can start using points if you want.

HIT UP REDDIT. Conflicting opinions abound on credit cards! One good place to find them is—drumroll please—Reddit! There's a subreddit devoted to credit card tips and tricks. I know Reddit has a scary reputation, but that segment of the site has great advice on getting your score up and updated information on which cards are the best for what. Just don't click around to any other subreddits. It's a rabbit hole. If you're not cozy with Reddit, you can go on the myFico forum, where people post advice on topics like student loans, car loans, mortgages, and of course, credit cards.

PATIENCE, YOUNG GRASSHOPPER. Once you apply for a card, you'll know within minutes if you've been approved (if the site has instant approval, which most do). The bank or company will pull your credit score, then ask your income and some other basic information to approve you and set your credit limit. (My credit limit on my Bank of America card is $5,000, while my credit limit on my American Express card, which I applied for while I was more financially solvent, is $10,000.) You can also apply for a credit card over the phone or by mail. Credit.com said if you're denied, the denier is legally required to send you a letter explaining why, which is obviously a super fun thing to get in the mail. Credit itself shows up on your credit report only six months after you start accruing it, so it may take time to build.

It won't surprise you to learn that The Points Guy is a die-hard credit card fan who believes people should not be using cash. He says cash is too easy to lose or have stolen. With cash, you won't get fraud or other protections, and you're not earning anything back. (I'm not sure my paranoid self agrees with this. I think you should have a mix of both.) He also thinks it's easier to track your finances with credit cards for budgeting and tax purposes. This is directly opposed to bipolar activist Julie Fast who needs cash to feel aware of what she's spent or my friends, like sex workers or undocumented people, who have to operate in a cash economy because of their jobs, circumstances, or lifestyles. Don't feel badly if you're more like Fast and my friends than you are like The Points Guy. Or maybe you're like me, falling somewhere in between.

TAKEAWAYS

- Credit cards CAN be dangerous if you use them to spend more than you can afford—especially due to high interest rates. (Know your interest rates!) Ideally you should use them just the way you would use cash (not spending more than you could reasonably pay back at some point) and paying them off on time.

- If you are a responsible credit card holder, you can have access to some really great perks like cash back, price rewind (a deal where if you find the thing you bought at a cheaper price, Citibank will refund you the difference), and travel insurance in case you lose your bags or your stuff is stolen or damaged while you're traveling. Some cards even come with roadside assistance.

- Scour reviews for cards, just as you would for buying a car or a mattress or a video game console.

- Decide if a credit card is for you at all. If, like a younger Gaby, you can't stop yourself from spending "imaginary" money, then credit cards might not be right for you yet. I'm still not great at this and regularly build up credit card debt that I have to work to pay down. I've accepted that this might just be never-ending for me. Old habits die hard. But awareness of that is a good percent of the battle.

9

A FAD DIET
FOR YOUR WALLET

Super popular budget guru Dave Ramsey tries to get his followers to save toward a $1,000 emergency fund that is not to be touched unless it's for a dire situation like a collapsed roof or an appendectomy. This is different from a "Mistakes" fund for cleaning up messes you've made for yourself, which many experts advocate for *on top of* a savings account, an emergency fund, and a retirement account. But the two are in the same family. Writer Paulette Perhach calls on women specifically to have an "F-Off Fund" for getting out of abusive relationships or leaving jobs where they're being harassed, let's say. These different savings funds are made from budgeting HARD.

Ramsey *really* believes in budgeting, which puts him at odds with another famous finance guru, Suze Orman. She believes budgeting is a fad diet that people don't ever stick to, and when they lose it, they binge hard. Orman, however, did recommend on Oprah's website in 2016 that when it comes to a budget, you should set aside $50 a month from your income for "treats." Everything else should go to "necessities."

Orman has fans, but Ramsey has DEVOTEES. There are endless Dave Ramsey followers on YouTube, where I spend a lot of my time. A trip down the Ramsey YouTube hole led me to a fascinating channel, "Life with Sarah." Sarah, a young woman based in Texas, said she learned to sacrifice big-time from Ramsey. She cut her cable, for example, and uses her videos to chronicle her strict budgeting in her life with her husband. Sarah's enthusiasm is infectious, and she's clearly very savvy, so I don't know how to feel about the extreme sparse lifestyle she preaches in Ramsey's name.

To be completely honest, hearing people talk about intense budgeting makes me nervous from a political standpoint. I think it's the idea that the proles are supposed to fix their problems with self-deprivation, giving up getting haircuts and coffee and snacks, so those prospering in the bankrupt capitalist system can keep bathing in calves' blood or whatever it is they do.

I'm not alone. One of these budget hounds' biggest critics is the author Helaine Olen, whose book *Pound Foolish* is subtitled *Exposing the Dark Side of the Personal Finance Industry*. I originally found Olen while looking up videos of Suze Orman, and Olen's criticism of Orman hit on a creeping doubt I'd been feeling in my heart.

Olen posits that condescending, overconfident experts like Orman and Ramsey are part of the machine that broke us, and now they make money selling the repair schematics back to us. They get richer and richer doling out conflicting bits of advice disguised as gospel, she said, and we pay for the pleasure of being told to cut back on coffee.

Being prudent with your money is all well and good, but what about the system we're living under that benefits only a select few? Budgeting implies the poorest of the poor have to spend less, so the richest of the rich can spend more (as I said, on all that calves' blood keeping them looking young).

Olen said in a 2013 *CBS News* interview, "All we want is someone to tell us what to do." It's very easy to fall under the spell of one of these gurus if you're floundering because you're exhausted and sad and someone is claiming to have a solution. Honestly, I get it. The number of times I've driven past a Scientology billboard during a deep depression and felt like, "Fuck it," is too high for me to judge anyone who worships Suze Orman or Dave Ramsey.

The commenters on the CBS video of Helaine Olen are split: some say she's promoting a victim mentality and others say that she is making money shitting on successful gurus out of jealousy or contrarianism. Others agree that the "shame and blame" inherent in not looking at the rising cost of insurance and medical bills and the disgusting stagnation of wages for the average person doesn't take into account the whole picture. I agree with Olen because I'm a *Mad Max: Fury Road* burn-it-all-down anarchist at my core. But I'm still trying to game this system I know is ugly. Olen thinks by encouraging people to give up their lattes rather than rioting at expensive health care, we're plugging a massive leak with a wine cork. "If you just learn this stuff, then we don't need the appropriate legislation to fix the problem," Olen says, mimicking financial gurus and the people who swear by them. I am what the youth call "shook."

———

What I consider "not a lot of money" has changed big time since I got a lump sum of about $50,000 for that TV show Allison and I sold in 2016. When that happened, I managed to put $19,000 into my savings account and told myself I wouldn't touch that money.

I've touched that money. My savings account now fluctuates between $5,000 and $10,000 depending on how closely I'm paying attention to my finances that month or what unexpected or emergency expenses have emerged. If it falls below that range, I stop and consider what I've been overspending on. Then I despair.

In the past, a $50,000 check would have made me feel like one of the Jenners. But now the responsibility of it makes me anxious and confused. I wasn't prepared. So much went to taxes. How did I spend nearly $5,000 in less than six months? Is it only because I had it that I suddenly felt okay to spend it? When I added another $5,000 of it into my retirement fund, I started worrying that it was too soon to start saving so much for retirement. What if I need that money?

You: For what, Gaby?

Me: I don't know. For things.

For almost thirty years, I never even had $5,000 in my bank account *collectively*, and now I've blown through that?! What has changed?

I haven't been buying myself jewels and furs, so what have I been buying? For the first time in my life, in 2017, I clicked on the "Budgeting" tab on my Bank of America account and voilà! There's an actual visual breakdown of my spending! Who knew!?

In the span of a random month in 2017, here were my expenditures:

- $1,239.61 for rent, which isn't bad for a one bedroom in Silverlake. I've lived here alone for 3½ years, something I never thought I'd be able to afford to do and *was* doing technically before I could actually afford to do it. In fact, I've paid my rent late enough times that my landlord doesn't accept checks from me. I have to pay each month's rent in a money order or cashier's check. (Sorry, Maria!)

- $276 for groceries. Investopedia.com said $500 per month per household on food in LA is average. Even adding random snacks, my total groceries cost me much less than that. My spending on restaurants varies wildly. Some months it's $100; this month it was $12 (a rare low for me).

- $223 for car insurance. When I first looked at it in 2017, Geico was charging me $559.85 a month for my car insurance. During the process of writing this book, I've been kicked off Geico for having three fender benders in one year (I'm the best) and now have Access for my car, which costs me $223 a month.

- $284.75 a month for health insurance.
- $400 on meds and therapy.
- $50 to Southern California Gas Company.
- $194 to Time Warner/Spectrum.
- $556 on student loans. In 2017, I was paying my three student loans: to Navient for $338 and two through Nelnet for $113 and $105 a month. In 2018, I paid off the smaller ones in full and now just pay $338 a month to Navient. (*Just.* LOL.)
- $62 on personal grooming. I'm an actress who is on camera, and I used to like to have gel finger-nails so they don't chip. At this point in my life, I usually got them redone every two weeks or so. Eventually I gave up getting my nails done entirely, and I don't miss it. (I also stopped dying my hair blonde, which saves me four hours and $300 every couple of months.) Not everyone can do that or wants to do that, but that's something that opened up some extra cash for me.
- $80 on parking meters and ride apps. When I lived in New York, I took the subway everywhere and had to factor in a MetroCard. Now I live in LA and I drive. I never, ever look at the parking meter. I slide my card. I hit accept, and I keep walking regardless of how much time I'll be spending at the venue. It seems silly, but maybe if I spent two seconds looking at how much parking was costing me and actually doing the math on how long I would be at this parking meter, I could save some money.

- $30 on ATM fees: ($2, $3 at a time) because I don't take out enough cash to carry around from an actual Bank of America ATM that won't charge me and instead run around popping into liquor stores to get cash whenever I instantly need it. I could maybe stand to go get enough cash for the week from the Bank of America on Monday and stop handing over small fees to these random ATMs.

- $600 on Amazon: Holy shit. Not every month is this bad, but man oh man! Speaking of impulsive idiocy! I impulse-buy books on subjects I express a passing whim in learning about or pins and hats to give as gifts to my friends or a humidifier for myself after seeing some Facebook video about how they can revitalize your whole sleep cycle. (I keep forgetting to use it.) I buy props like wigs and easels for my YouTube channel when I could just borrow them from friends. I buy movies to watch while I eat lunch because I work from home. This is plainly unacceptable.

- $100 on coffee, juice, and beer. (I've since cut out beer.)

- $65 on clothes and shoes. I'm not much of a shopper, and I don't particularly care about trends and fashion. (Awesome for you if you, like my girlfriend, super care! I just never got into it.) This is a high amount on clothes for me.

- $200 on subscription services: Spotify/Netflix/Amazon Prime/Dropbox, etc.

- $40 on gym membership: This is actually a steal!
- $60 on gas: This varies depending on how much I drive a month.
- $180 to charities like Planned Parenthood, medical GoFundMes, the Standing Rock protests, and the LA LGBT center. Some are monthly, some one time.

Looking at the actual figures broken down that way, I can't believe how much money I spend in both checking and on credit cards. When I never had more than $500 in my bank account at once, I couldn't fathom that I'd spend $65 on clothing and not even notice. Or that my rent would be so casually past the thousands. (In NYC, I struggled to find places under $800 every time I moved because I could not afford to go above that; in fact, I could barely afford that. In Boston, my rent limit was $500.) Or that I'd pay for two movies on Amazon in one week and then never watch either of them.

After studying these figures, I decided not to create a monthly budget for myself. I know that, like Suze Orman suggested, I won't stick to it long term. Instead, at my girl-friend's suggestion, I downloaded two apps: One is called Digit, which is a mix between a budgeting app and a savings app. I created different funds to save for different expenses, and then every day, Digit takes a dollar or a few cents, depending on how much money I have, out of my account and slips it into one of these funds. I hardly notice the missing pennies.

While it's not a huge, strict overhaul like Ramsey would

suggest, going through my bank account and looking at what I spend on did motivate me to separate my extraneous expenses into these smaller accounts. When I need money for a haircut, for instance, I can look at my haircut account and see if I can afford it. This has been a huge help. Budgeting, like all other things money, isn't one size fits all. So let's look at some of the different ways people budget.

BUDGETING THEORIES

CASH ONLY. In 2017, writer Kathleen Elkins did an eight-week "cash diet" that consisted of surviving on $60 a week (for anything other than rent and bills). She wrote about it for CNBC in January, offering her tips on budgeting: (1) Track all your spending in an Excel spreadsheet, (2) cook your own food and stop drinking alcohol out—or, hell, quit drinking altogether, (3) set a specific numbered goal so that when you spend $5 on a whim, you can know that's $5 less to spend on something else, and (4) socialize without spending tons of money. (It took me YEARS to realize I could hang out with friends at bars without buying a drink every half-hour. You can get a ginger ale instead of a $14 cocktail. Don't be embarrassed if you're the only one.) You can bring snacks to the park! You can go to a free museum! You can go for a walk or bike ride! My girlfriend and I like to shoot hoops at the outdoor court in our neighborhood. So many activities are free!

ENVELOPE MONEY. The Envelope Budget, according to TheBalance.com, requires you to take a chunk of money out in cash and separate it into envelopes marked for what it's going to be spent on. "When you run out of money in that category, you stop spending," the article said. "In order to make this work, you cannot use your debit card for the categories that you have envelopes for." This method seems super hard to me, but if you can swing it, I bow to you.

50/30/20. The 50/30/20 budget suggests that "needs" get 50 percent of your income, "wants" get 30 percent, and 20 percent goes into savings, retirement, and debt repayment. This is a good benchmark if you don't want to track every dollar of every category, but it's not necessarily realistic if you live in a super high-rent place where that alone could be half your income, even with roommates. What about other needs like bills or food? It doesn't leave much room.

CATEGORY 5. This budget breaks your income into five parts. For housing, you can spend up to 35 percent of your income. For transportation, you should spend no more than 15 percent of your income. For other living expenses (such as groceries, utilities, and wants), you can spend up to 25 percent of your income. For savings, you should set aside 10 percent each month. And for debt payoff, 15 percent of your income, according to the Balance.

You can also use specific budgeting apps, like the second app I downloaded at my girlfriend's behest, called "You Need A Budget." This app works for me because my income is different every month. It allows me to see how much I spend every month so I can plan for expenses instead of being surprised by every bill. I can also clearly see how much money I have left over and what categories (restaurants, movies, clothes) it can reasonably be put into. I like seeing the numbers go up and down based on what money I choose to use or save. There are literally a gajillion different budgeting apps for both iPhone and Android. Here are six other popular choices and their pros and cons:

MINT INTUIT

Pros: The OG budgeting app. Links all your bank accounts and investments. Free to use. Provides credit score and tips to improve it. Shows you a pie chart of earned versus spent and what you spent it on.

Cons: Has ads. You create your own categories, which can be time-consuming and cluttered. Not a very user-friendly interface, in my opinion.

BUDGET CALENDAR

Pros: Color-coded. You can plan up to twenty years in the future. It also provides data on how much to pay, and for how long, until a debt is completely paid off.

Cons: Tracks expenses by the date you manually enter them and whether they're one time or recurring, so it won't track your entire income. It's not Android compatible.

MY DAILY BUDGET

Pros: You can see how much you are spending every day so you're not caught off-guard at the end of the month. You can also input your expenses and income, and then the app will tell you exactly how much money you can spend each day.

Cons: The premium version is expensive (up to $4! For an app!). This works better if you have a fixed income.

EVERY DOLLAR

Pros: Free, basic. Manually enter all your spending into customized categories so you have to confront what you're spending. It has no frills, and the emphasis is on a balance between income and spending.

Cons: Some features cost money. Founded by Dave Ramsey so some of the products pushed on you are Ramsey specific. It's time-consuming to input every expense by hand because you have to enter everything down to the, you guessed it, dollar.

CLARITY MONEY

Pros: It can help you cancel unwanted accounts or unused memberships, provides discounts and coupons, can reach out to providers and negotiate to lower your bills, helps you save for big-ticket specific items, and provides your credit score. It also has cool pie charts.

Cons: Takes a one-third commission for any negotiating on your behalf. It works best if you have a steady income you can input (no freelancing) and is better for monitoring spending habits than for budgeting.

EXCEL

Pros: Old faithful. Excel is REALLY no frills; it's just a spreadsheet service that comes with your computer. Before all these apps, many people used it to keep track of their finances without all those annoying bells and whistles.

Cons: All manual, baby.

TAKEAWAYS

- The gurus can provide a path, but you can't live your whole life doing everything these megarich preachers tell you to do, even if they seem aspirational. They make money off your devotion and sacrifice. While you scrounge, they fly private. Keep that in mind.
- Go through your bank statements and make a list of what you spend on, and exactly how much you spend on it. See what seems like too much for your liking.

Don't lose the stuff you love, but lose some stuff you don't need. (Again, $600 on Amazon?! Kill me.)

- There's no right way to budget, nor do you have to "budget" at all in the typical sense of the word. But you have to be sure that what you spend is compatible with your income.

- You can go for a super fancy app, or kick it old school with a spreadsheet.

- Mark on a calendar when your bills come out of your account and how much they are, so you'll never be surprised again.

10

THE TAX (WO)MAN

Because I'm considered a freelancer and now make more money than I've ever made in the past, my taxes were a whopping $10,000 this year. This had never happened to me before. Usually I got a refund, or if I had to pay anything, I'd go on a payment plan to pay it off in small amounts. When I expressed shock that my taxes were now so high, Allison laughed at me: "You've had money for one day, and you're already a Republican." (That was before I learned about all the great stuff taxes pay for—for example, roads, schools, infrastructure, food stamps, and other government assistance. I am sorry for my initial reaction.)

I had a lot to learn about taxes. In 2016, my accountant Dan Frattali told me to go through my bank statements for the previous year to see what would be possible to write off. I'd never done this before, and I kept procrastinating because

I just didn't want to do it. I drank cold coffee. I replied to my friend Alexis on Twitter. I stood up and walked around. I thought about putting on socks. I would have rather had someone break into my apartment and punch me in the face so I could deal with the immediate fallout of *that* rather than continue to go through these bank statements.

Taxes make my brain explode. Even the breakdown in *Personal Finance for Dummies* is too confusing for me. (What does that make *me*?)

Here's what I've discovered in my research:

Because I live in California, I pay both state income and federal income taxes. My parents in Florida pay only federal because Florida is one of a few states that doesn't have a state income tax. (They love that.) *Dummies* says you should try to minimize the amount of taxes you pay by reducing your taxable income or increasing your deductions. Deductions are decreases to your taxable income that come in the form of expenses, especially expenses that resulted in more income—for example, writing off business travel or lunches with clients. These can be removed from how much you end up paying in taxes. The Internal Revenue Service (IRS) also provides incentives and perks for positive money behaviors like saving for retirement.

Accountant Dan loads me with information come tax time, and though he talks slowly like a very patient teacher, I still like to record our meetings so I can listen back later. Recording meetings is a good trick if the other party is comfortable with it. I was embarrassed to ask at first, but it's even more embarrassing to nod, pretending you comprehend what you need to do, and then totally flake on following up. At one of our first in-person meetings at his office in Westwood, I asked him how many people my age are actually sitting down to do all of this versus ignoring it completely. He said that in his experience as a financial advisor, it's a mix of both.

The IRS must know no one is keeping track of their shit. (Am I asking to be audited? I'm kidding, IRS! I keep track of everything! We all do!) Before 2016, I'd just take a bunch of tax-related papers to H&R Block. (You can also use online tax services like TurboTax, but those always intimidated me.) I had no idea what deductions I was writing off, what deductions I *could* write off, what the accountant at H&R Block was doing to calculate said write-offs, and what papers I even needed to be turning in. It was all a mess.

Here's what I found out about that paperwork:

WHAT IS A W-2?

A W-2 is a form you receive from your employer and fill out as a full-time employee to indicate how much in taxes will be withheld from your paycheck. Depending on the numbers you put in, you can either get your full salary and pay a lump sum in taxes, or you can have wages withheld, and when tax time comes, you might get back a refund. You get a refund if the government decides it took too much out of your check weekly. That lump sum is a weird financial apology.

Which is better? It depends on your income and lifestyle. When I was getting regular paychecks in NYC, I would usually get my wages taken out for taxes upfront and receive a lower salary every week. Then I'd be pleasantly surprised at the end of the year by my refund. But because I'm an irresponsible person, I would be so excited by my lump sum that I would spend it immediately to cover my year of irresponsibility. My usual salary was too low so I'd spend all year putting off a lot of things I needed, like doctors' appointments or new boots. The lump sum paid for that. The flip side was that I wasn't saving, so if I didn't put down deductions on my W-2 initially, I was screwed come tax season if I needed to make any additional tax payments.

When I started working full time at Buzzfeed, a major corporation, I didn't know anything about filling out a W-2. I randomly claimed no deductions and turned in the form. I was too embarrassed to ask for help because it seemed like something I should already know. I figured if something was wrong, HR would just tell me to fill it out "correctly." Not so. Every couple of weeks, I was delighted by how much I was taking home. I eventually showed my coworker and then-boyfriend my paycheck. His eyes grew wide. We were making the same salary, but he was taking home much less. His expression said, "You're gonna be fucked on taxes." He was right. I owed $700.

That's when I called the IRS, terrified, and asked about a payment plan. I don't love talking on the phone, especially with government employees. I worried the employee would laugh in my face and then drain my bank account and hold my cat as collateral for what I couldn't afford. The IRS sounded scary and evil. Why invite them into my life? In reality, the conversation was mundane. The IRS employee on the phone asked me what I thought I could reasonably pay each month and I meekly said, "Fifty dollars?" I was completely unsure if that was an okay number or if she'd yell at me for being a ne'er-do-well. The woman on the phone did not react at all. I was not the only person making this request. I probably wasn't even in the top 100 of people asking for small recurring payments. It was a comforting and depressing thought.

WHAT IS A W-9?

A W-9 is a tax form usually used by independent contractors. It's not one you turn into the IRS. You get it from your employers and they use it to keep track of your name, address, and taxpayer identification number after you turn it back in to them. The W-9 is used by the company to create your 1099 so they (and you) can report your income to the IRS come tax time. A W-9 can be downloaded from the official IRS website.

If you have people working for you, you could ask them to fill one out. If you're working as a freelancer or consultant, the company you're working for will give you a standard blank 1099 before you start so you can put in your name and Social Security number. (Because the form has this sensitive information, think twice about emailing it or to whom you send it.)

WHAT IS A 1099?

Ah, my old friend the 1099! This one is for freelancers and is sent to you by the company paying you. It's one of the papers you have to bring to the accountant or H&R Block in your accordion folder of random papers and receipts. (Just me?)

If you have a day job, then this is for any income you make outside it. My entire income is freelance. This makes taxes a nightmare because instead of calculating deductions from one place, Accountant Dan calculates them from every publication I wrote for once, every acting gig or TV job, every branded deal on the YouTube channel, and every small task I did and forgot about until the 1099s come in the mail. A big help would have been to keep track of all the jobs I did in that year, something I have never done.

WHAT I SHOULD HAVE DONE

According to my accountant, this is what I should have done.

ALWAYS KEEP A CALENDAR

Since I was in the third grade, I've kept a paper planner where I write down my whole schedule at the beginning of every week. I'm also neurotic, so once a task is completed, I scratch it out in pen. I was 28 when my manager, Matt, insisted I get a Google calendar. Before that, if I didn't have my trusty paper planner with me, I had no idea what I was doing that day or what I had done as recently as the day before.

Don't be like me. Keeping any kind of planner (without crossing stuff out) will remind you of things you can write off—like "business lunches" (which has a broad definition in Los Angeles). I have a lot of friends who joke that every time we get lunch, they're writing it off. But is it a joke? Are they really keeping track of and writing off every lunch?

When my accountant asked me to look over the past year, all I had were some vague ideas about what I'd done: gigs, meetings, writing assignments. Be better than me. Keep a readable calendar with all your events during the year.

KEEP TRACK OF THINGS LIKE THESE

HOW YOU USE YOUR CAR

How many miles do you drive a year, and for what purpose? How many times a month do you fill up your gas tank? How much do you pay in insurance? Any repairs, car washes, DMV fees?

WHAT YOU SPEND ON YOUR HEALTH

I'm an actress (sometimes), so Dan said I *might* be able to deduct my gym and my therapist (that has nothing to do with being an actress—*or does it?*). Medications can sometimes be deducted. Differing sources say birth control might be a deduction depending on what it's used for. Keep track of all of your health care spending.

ANYTHING YOU SPEND ON YOUR BUSINESS

Purchases made while on the road for business are deductible, so I should keep track of them. Save restaurant and coffee receipts. Save receipts for Ubers, for picking up extra toothpaste, and for anything else bought while out of town. There are apps where you can save digital photos of your receipts so you're not carrying paper around. My friend Myq keeps a folder on his iPhone of just photos of receipts while he travels for stand-up comedy. He was doing this before the apps were invented, so he missed out on being a millionaire, I guess.

If I attend a comedy show to scout new talent for my You-Tube channel, Dan said, I can probably write off the ticket price. Great. Now comedy shows are work related! Dan said if I subscribe to any magazines or trade publications, I can write those off too. He also suggested I keep track of visits to Office Depot and Staples because those are often work related as well.

DONATIONS

I currently donate to several causes. (Thanks so much, 2016 election!) I give to the LA LGBT Center, Standing Rock, Planned Parenthood, and several individual medical GoFund-Mes. You can write off donations, but Dan said mine would have to add up to $6,800 altogether in order for them to make a difference (this threshold number is different for everyone, and subject to change as Trump's new tax plan goes into effect). I'm shocked to see that the GoFundMes I donate to are not tax deductible because the IRS recognizes only "qualified charitable organizations." Instead, most GoFundMe donations are considered "personal gifts." (What the hell?)

TaxGirl writer Kelly Erb wrote in a column from 2015: "If you're not sure whether an organization is qualified, ask to see their letter from the Internal Revenue Service (IRS): many organizations will actually post their letters on their website."

BE READY FOR THIS TO TAKE A WHILE

I sat with Dan for a half day working on my taxes the first time, and since then have spent even more time with him, poring over receipts and bank statements. (I see floating numbers around his face in my nightmares.) Getting into the weeds of your spending like this takes hours to do, but it's worth it since it can save you a lot of cash money, some of which you can then spend on a bottle of wine to heal you from the trauma of doing your taxes. The better organized you are, the easier this process will be each year.

TAKEAWAYS

- Taxes are confusing and complicated for almost everyone. You're not deficient for not understanding them.
- Keeping track of your expenses now will save you time and headaches in the future.
- There's a reason accountants and tax help websites exist: You're not meant to do this alone. Don't be shy about asking for help from professionals, your family members, your friend's mom, or the myriad apps and websites just for taxes. It's an entire industry.

TEN OTHER THINGS IRS COULD STAND FOR

1. I'm Really Stressful

2. Irritating Reality System

3. Irate Restless Superiors

4. I've Ruined Something

5. I Rightfully Suck

6. It's Reaching Sadism

7. Indignant Realistic Sadness

8. Immediately Really Shitty

9. Ignorance Required Sometimes

10. It Rarely Smiles

11

MY LOVE DON'T COST A THING

When I'm interested in a new person romantically, my best friend always asks me what the person does for work, and I always resent the question. It's not very exciting to think about the finances of someone you're lusting over. "Why don't you ask me about their radiant smile?" "Or their quick sense of humor?" "Or their adorable pet hedgehog?"

The first time I realized money might factor into a relationship was when I was 24 years old. It was toward the end of my time living in New York City. I freelanced as a day job and then spent the rest of my time at the People's Improv Theater, where I performed on one of the house teams. Improv can be a haven for forever-children: adults who don't want to, or really can't, grow up. In a "comedy pyramid scheme," you had to pay hundreds of dollars to finish level 5 of the courses the theater requires you to take just to audition to do improv for free every week. (The theater charged patrons to attend, but I never saw any of that money.) The first round of classes, my grandmother Meme paid for as a birthday gift. It was about $400 for eight weeks. The second, third, fourth, and fifth rounds of classes must have gone on my credit card.

Being on an improv team required showing up to shows and rehearsals. My teammates and I paid for a coach and a rehearsal space out of pocket, pooling our money in the pre-Venmo days of cash. That was a job that paid in "stage time," much the way my freelance writing gigs paid in "exposure."

The Netflix animated show *BoJack Horseman* did a great episode basically comparing improv to a cult. Specifically, what it shares with most cults is the people who are most drawn to it are the ones who have no money.

My story was classic New York: I started dating a fellow improviser. He was, like a lot of the other men at the theater, a good amount older than I was, had no steady day job, and was in tons of debt. I was maniacally attracted to him.

He was the first person I dated who was vocally judgmental of my financial connection to my parents. My Bank of America account was linked to theirs and they periodically used my account as if it was one of their own, funneling money in and out. At 24, I didn't see anything wrong with that. My money was their money and their money was my money. When I revealed this information to my boyfriend, he expressed grave concern.

"You need to get your own bank account that they can't access," he said. (My friend Lauren also chastised me when I told her this story. She's had her own bank account since she was 15.)

My parents were concerned that this guy's ultimate plan was to take me away from them and "money independence" was his excuse. They fought back against my opening my own bank account, which might not have occurred to me to do without this man's influence, but also now seemed obviously overdue. I felt guilty about getting my own account, but I did it.

The problem was this older dude, and the ones around me who loved to give me advice on how to be an adult, were not financially independent themselves. I was surrounded by people, mostly male comedians, stuck in arrested development. It seemed normal that well into your 30s, you'd be out partying all night with nothing in your savings account. I didn't understand how these people made money. How could one of the 35-year-old guys I drank with afford to live in a condo downtown by himself but never have a job to speak of?

My then-boyfriend was deep in credit card debt, a sentence I barely understood. I spent a lot of time googling "what it means to marry someone with debt." The results were terrifying. Many op-eds advised against it. My mom, a divorce attorney, advised against it. Money, she warned, is the number one reason for divorce.

"You start off the marriage behind the eight ball," she said. "You can't build a life. How do you save for a house? How do you travel?" She also worried about my marrying someone in credit card debt because "it shows irresponsibility and not being realistic about your lifestyle." (I don't know if I agree with this, but she's a concerned mom.)

Ed, a 50-year-old retired software engineer from Hong Kong, told me in a phone interview that he makes good money. When he married his wife, she had no job but no debt either. Two years into their marriage, she became very sick, the result of a chronic illness she'd been battling all her life. Her long stay in the hospital threw her into $12,000 of unexpected debt. His wife, he said, wanted to pay back the medical debt entirely on her own. After all, she was the one who got sick; it wasn't fair to make her husband pay it back. He said they argued about it for a while. As her husband and someone who could afford the debt with no problem, Ed insisted he take care of it. He said they compromised, and his wife paid half of it.

Does marrying someone imply all debt—credit card, medical, student loan—is a collective problem now (to be together "for richer or for poorer," as it were)? The issue of one spouse having debt that the other one isn't necessarily responsible for could cause a lot of resentment for a less emotionally and financially secure couple. Ed and his wife's situation came as a surprise to them, but what about if you're marrying someone who already has debt? What if one partner is better off but certainly doesn't have enough to cover any of their spouse's debts?

———

HuffPost senior relationships editor Ashley Rockman, who got married in September 2016, says that because student loans are so common today, debt shouldn't necessarily be an automatic deal breaker. It *is* incredibly important, however, that your potential partner has a concrete plan in place for paying it off. If your partner has debt and either isn't working to pay it off or doesn't seem to understand the gravity of owing large sums of money, that's a huge red flag. It could also indicate problematic personality traits that might cause issues down the road.

Before she was the relationships editor, Rockman, 30, oversaw *HuffPost*'s Divorce section. She said the experience showed her that tying yourself to someone in the eyes of the government is more than just a fairy tale. It's a legal contract like any other.

My mom, the divorce and child custody attorney, agreed: "I have had people decide not to marry as a result of the pre-nup negotiations because they get to see another side of the other person," she said. My mom is a major advocate for the pre-nuptial agreement, a contract made before a wedding or civil union that includes specifics of spousal support or division of assets in the event of a separation or divorce. (Fun fact: If you decide to sign this sort of contract after you wed, that's called a post-nuptial agreement.) A pre-nup, she said, allows each of you to remain in control of your financial lives. If you get divorced without this agreement, a judge you don't know gets to dictate your future based on a set of laws that are often unfair and don't take into account the particular circumstances of your life.

My mom would kill me if I ever got married without a pre-nup, but some people find them very "unromantic." A *HuffPost* blog post from 2015, "Why You Shouldn't Sign a Prenup," provides maybe the most ludicrous "romantic" argument against a pre-nup I'd ever heard. The blogger wrote that "the act of getting one is by its very nature pernicious to relationships." She claimed pre-nups encouraged couples not to try as hard to save their marriages because there are no stakes if separation is easy. In other words, having a pre-nup doesn't incentivize the couple to stay together. This is bad advice, and I've heard *a lot* of bad advice. A couple's commitment to staying together should be about more than the inconvenience of divorce, and sometimes, divorce is the best-case scenario. People use divorce to extract themselves from toxic or abusive situations, which can be made even more challenging when money is involved. (I had a friend who stayed with a cheating fiancé because she couldn't afford to move out.) Many of the women my mom has represented were so relieved after their divorce was finalized that they invited her out for celebratory drinks.

Rockman relayed the story of a couple who spent ten horrifying years in divorce court fighting over custody specifics because they had three kids. Had they had a pre-nup in place outlining what happened if they divorced— alimony, custody, child support—they could have saved a lot of money and time. Instead, they endured years of lawyers' fees, emotional exhaustion, court dates, and all kinds of other consequences.

Rockman says that while marriage can certainly be romantic, it is also a contract, which means that it should be approached in the same way you'd approach an auto loan or a mortgage: with serious forethought, attention to detail, and cautionary provisions put into place that might become necessary should circumstances change.

In my relationship with my fellow improviser, I paid for a lot that I couldn't afford. I bought us food and drinks, clothes, yoga classes, gifts, and drugs. I didn't want something as petty as money to stop us from taking adorable couple photos in fun places. I didn't want to have to think about finances while falling in love. (I'm sure many people don't.)

In 2013, I even tried to pay for us to move to Los Angeles together. I floated the idea that since he had family in that city, maybe he could move in with them at first and then eventually move in with me. I wanted to rescue him from the bad habits he had developed in New York, one of the most expensive cities in the United States. He vaguely acknowledged my proposal, but nothing firm was decided. When I moved to LA in August, he said he'd follow me in October. In mid-October, we met up at a wedding in Atlanta (Who do you think paid for the plane tickets???), where we finally broke up.

———

I was 25 and heartbroken in LA. In my lonely desperation, I made a terrible mistake: I started casually dating a famous person who slid into my DMs on Twitter. (It's 2018 as I write this, and I think I can safely say: *Never ever date a famous man. Ever.*)

Coming off my relationship with the improviser, it was jarring to be dating this new wealthy guy whom I'll call "Roman Holiday"—after the Gregory Peck–Audrey Hepburn romantic comedy about a princess (him) who falls in love with a working-class reporter (me). He was the spoiled Hepburn character, learning about the joys of the simple life outside the castle through the eyes of me, Peck's working man. Roman had been famous since he was a teenager and was annoyingly clueless about what was affordable for most people. One time, I texted him that I'd shown up early to meet a friend at the mall and I wasn't sure what to do with my extra time. He suggested that I go into the Apple store and buy myself something to play with.

Roman owned multiple homes. He had sweatpants that cost hundreds of dollars. He was older than me and more successful, and he abused the power imbalance in our relationship to make me very insecure. Dating him as a non-rich person, I felt pressure to present myself as if I were above my station. I wore high heels more often. I got my hair done whenever I thought we would see each other. I scrutinized my wardrobe, suddenly unsure about the strings coming off my cheap Forever 21 outfits. (Seriously, why do they always have strings?)

I learned that while dating someone with no money made me spend more, dating someone with a lot of money ALSO made me spend more. One of the reasons my relationship with Roman ended is that he started secretly dating another woman, a fellow famous person who was wealthy like him. (I found out we were broken up when he showed up on a red carpet with her. Like I said, NEVER EVER DATE A FAMOUS MAN.) I don't know how much being in the same economic bracket affected their relationship, but I imagine it probably made it easier for them to understand each other. Maybe it's simpler to date within your financial sphere.

———

After two relationships with two men of very different financial means, I started dating a feminine woman who was still looking for a post-college job. I didn't have a disposable income, but I felt an obligation to take care of her the way I cared for my improviser ex. (Fatal flaw: I love a project.)

Even though neither of us was a cisgender man and we could have avoided classic gender roles, I subconsciously decided (without asking her) that I should take on the more traditional masculine "provider" role. I believed in her and thought, "Eventually we'll be on the same playing field, and it'll all be fine." I was further along in my career and making more money, but I wasn't anywhere near financially stable. It started to stress me out to be responsible for someone else when I was just becoming responsible for myself, even though she never asked me to do that. Money came between us without us ever actually talking about it.

Attempting to break my shaky streak, I then dated a woman in her 30s who was successful in her career. We were on a level playing field. She could pay for stuff as often as I could. She was also more masculine than me, and so in the beginning, she expected to pay for me by default. She was always shocked when I pulled out my wallet. I asked her why she thought she had to pay for me, and she said she hadn't ever thought about it too hard. Perhaps it was because I was presenting more femininely then. She just assumed she would pay even though we made a similar amount of money. She saw herself as "the dude." (That, again, is a shame because the best part of queer woman dating is there are no dudes. Write that down.)

After she and I split, I started noticing a pattern when I'd go on dates to restaurants with other women. When it came time to hand over the check, the server would give it to the more traditionally masculine of the two of us. Then, no matter who paid and who handed the check back to the server (regardless of gender), the server would hand the check back to the "masculine" person, assuming that's who was paying.

When I polled Twitter on the topic, 37 percent of the 2,300 people who responded to the poll said that in their experience, "the butch one" was always handed the check. User PossibilityLeft wrote, "Not only do they always hand it to me, I'm side-eyed if my femme gf pays instead." Many people who replied said the check was usually left in the middle, and former wait staff largely agreed that this was typical restaurant policy. But in my experience, the check is always handed to "the butch one." It's good to know stereotypical gender roles exist even in non-normative relationships. (JK, it sucks.)

——————

I met my next serious boyfriend while working at Buzz-feed in 2015. My salary was higher than his, but as we got to know each other, I realized the more crucial difference was our completely opposite money scripts. I was a reckless spender, and he was a meticulous saver. He came from a wealthy family. My joke was that he looked like the type of guy who would tell a minimum-wage employee, "My father will hear about this." (This wasn't what he was like in real life at all, but his button-nose and deep-set eyes made him seem adorably snobbish.)

Because of our different backgrounds, there were severe money blindspots between us. He didn't take out loans for college. His family owned multiple properties. But if the saying goes that "rich people have the luxury of never having to think about money," then he was, in practice, not that. He thought about money a lot. He saved money. He had investments. He knew to negotiate his salary. This was not how I thought about money, and I thought about money a lot too.

He'd left a cushy job in finance to become a writer, but not without careful consideration. He was able to take that career risk by saving A LOT beforehand. I'd come out to LA with next to nothing, no plan, and a job that didn't pay well, and I was living in a small apartment with someone sleeping in the living room to offset the price of our rent. He, meanwhile, had moved into a house with three other roommates. He could have afforded to live alone but decided instead to save that money. I couldn't understand his thinking. My philosophy was once you have the money, you spend the money immediately to make your life more comfortable. Why squirrel it away while you live a less-than-ideal life?

When I visited his family's winter home, I was shocked to learn it was empty most of the year. Joking with his parents (but also semiserious), I asked if I could live there rent free. While we were together, he gifted me $3,000, no strings attached, to help get me out of a hole I'd dug for myself because of car repairs. I asked if I ever had to pay it back, and he said he honestly would not miss the money. To his credit, after we split up, he never tried to get that money back. He really did not need it.

During our relationship, he felt he had to rescue me: the same pressure I'd felt with the people I dated who were mak-

ing less than me. And in the end, that same stress contributed
to our breakup, just the other way around.

———

Though it can be easier to date someone who has a similar
money situation or at least a similar script, I don't mean
to imply that it's impossible to date outside your financial
sphere. It's all about maturity and patience. If handled well,
a couple's money differences should be a source of balance in
the relationship. Just as with any of your other differences—
cultural, religious, or otherwise—this is yet another way that
you can learn from each other.

This is what I've witnessed with my friend, director Carly
Usdin, who is a spender, and her wife, photographer Robin
Roemer, who is a saver. Carly said being with Robin has provided her financial accountability that she didn't have when
she was single. "Robin has absolutely made me want to plan
for the future." She added that she's definitely better with
money now than when she first met her wife.

On the flip side, Robin said that being with Carly encouraged her to treat herself to things she really needs. "She helps
me with the guilt I have after we go on a trip or I buy something nice," she said. "She talks me off that ledge."

So while money is an important thing to be on the same
page about in a relationship, it can also be illuminating to
date someone with different qualities than yours if you can
ensure that you'll be honest, willing to compromise, and
good influences on each other's spending and saving.

My Buzzfeed ex taught me to be much smarter with

money. It's to his credit that I now pay an incredibly low amount on rent. When I used to talk about making more money and moving somewhere better, my ex would steer me away from that idea, saying, "As you make more money, save it, and don't change your lifestyle." In Judd Apatow's book *Sick in the Head*, comedian Sarah Silverman says she does the same thing. Despite her success, she still rents a small apartment in LA and has intentionally never moved anywhere more lavish. I hold my ex's—and Silverman's—advice close to my heart. It was only once we split up that I realized how much of an influence he'd had on me—forcing me to make more responsible choices (which I'm sure he'd be thrilled to hear, if he ever wanted to talk to me again).

Rockman, the *HuffPost* relationships editor, said all couples need to discuss finances once the relationship gets serious, ideally even before then, rather than assuming it'll all magically work out. She gave the example of one partner believing spending $500 on a purse was no big deal while the other wasn't raised to spend that way, or even smaller examples, like one partner saving money by bringing lunch to work every day and the other always paying for lunch at a restaurant. Rockman, who's been with her partner for thirteen years, said sometimes you don't think a small money habit will bother you until it eats at you over time.

Another consideration as a couple is the degree to which you will be splitting expenses. Will expenses be split evenly, or prorated according to how much each person earns? Will they be pooled into one pot of money everyone can use? I'd argue for prorating by earnings as long as the person making more money doesn't resent the person making less. This way, no one's income is being unfairly drained, that is, neither partner has to "live up" or "live down" to what the other can afford.

Kristin F. Jones, a licensed marriage and family therapist in Los Angeles, advises couples to consider that money isn't the only currency in a relationship. A comedian couple I know told me that in the beginning of their relationship, when one of them made more money, the other took care of all household chores, including laundry and cleaning. This arrangement greatly reduced their stress and allowed both to contribute significantly to the relationship. The larger earner said she appreciated her partner doing the stuff she wasn't around to do, and it meant more to her than splitting expenses evenly.

Contributions are not just financial, so think about more than just money when combining finances and choosing how to split expenses. Other forms of labor count too.

TAKEAWAYS

- Dating is hard, especially when it comes to spending money on a partner. Try not to make assumptions about someone's situation based on background or gender, and don't put on a money front you can't maintain.
- Talk openly with serious partners about money. This doesn't have to be a scary "show me you can keep me in the manner I am accustomed to" or a "I am terrible at money and you should run far away" talk. You can

discuss your family's background or what your priorities would be if you suddenly were given $100,000. A hypothetical like the latter can help you get a sense of each other's attitudes toward money.

- Money is not super romantic, but it can have a huge impact on relationships. You don't want to wait a long time to find out you have no common ground on which to build a life together.

THINGS I HAVE BOUGHT FOR PEOPLE WHO ARE ABOUT TO DUMP ME

I have a history of buying expensive gifts for people I feel are about to dump me. It's a terrible plan. If I get a whiff that the person might be on their way out the door, I try to delay this by paying for something that will force that person to stay—for example:

Tickets to a Ratatat concert that I later had to sell on Craigslist when the dude dumped me anyway

A plane ticket from NYC to a wedding in Georgia at which the person dumped me (you knew about this one already, but that doesn't make it less hurtful!)

A $400 watch (my sole comfort is that this person continues to think of me while wearing it)

A custom necklace with the girl's cats' names on it (though to be fair, I broke up with her *after* I bought her that; guilt is just as motivating as panic for overspending on a dying relationship)

A new winter coat from Betsey Johnson (we were breaking up, sure, but I didn't want her to freeze to death!)

You can't stave off a breakup with money unless you are a billionaire Scientologist and your wife is trapped in a harrowing financial arrangement with you.

12

HERE COMES THE BILL

The closest I've come to my wedding was my bat mitzvah in 2001.

Throughout middle school, I attended a different bar or bat mitzvah party every weekend—sometimes twice a weekend. For these lavish parties, we not only had to buy expensive gifts for these new "adults," we were also expected to buy a new dress for every party (which I definitely couldn't always afford to do, to my utmost mortification). It was abundantly clear who could afford to do all this and who couldn't. Bar mitzvahs became a "my super sweet sixteen" nightmare, a competition for which parent could throw the most outrageous party for their thirteen-year-old child. I attended bar and bat mitzvah parties on boats and in high-profile nightclubs in Miami. Parents hired well-known party planners for these events, and some of them featured huge chocolate fountains and ice luges.

By stark contrast, the non-wealthy kids had bar and bat mitzvah parties that were small or (gasp!) more focused on religion, or maybe they didn't have one at all. This period of my youth messed with me hard—and not just with me but with my mom too.

As I approached the end of seventh grade and my own bat mitzvah closed in on us, my mom felt guilty about not being able to give me a party that would impress everyone at school. In her desperation, relying on her signature "act now, think later" mentality, she planned one we could not afford.

It was outrageous.

My theme was "outer space." The venue was decorated to look like a rocket. My centerpieces were spinning planets. We gave out personalized yarmulkes and apparel that said "Gabrielle's Galaxy." We hired professional dancers who came dressed as aliens and astronauts. In short, it was way more than any thirteen-year-old should ever be allowed to have. When I asked her about it in 2016, my mom blamed "peer pressure," and then she revealed the big number: My bat mitzvah cost our family $20,000! She told me we saved some money for it, and both my grandmothers helped out, but a chunk definitely went on credit cards. *Oy gevalt.*

I balk over the numbers, but the memories are what matter most to my mom. Every time we talk about this party, she reminds me how, at the end of the night, I lay on the floor in my dress, not wanting to take it off because if I took it off, then "it was really over." She cherishes that. It was priceless to her. Still, I can't believe my parents spent $20,000 on a thirteen-year-old's birthday party. Maybe it's because of this experience that I've never cared about a wedding. Been there, done that, have the yarmulkes to prove it.

Yet I've only actually been to four weddings as an adult. A lot of what I know about them comes from movies like *My Best Friend's Wedding*, which I was weirdly obsessed with in the fourth grade—not because I wanted to get married, but because I liked the singing and had a crush on Julia Roberts (who looks kind of like my mom; dissect *that*, people). I was shocked when a badass feminist writer friend told me once at dinner how she thought about her own wedding a lot. Weren't we not supposed be into that? (Trick question: Feminism is about choice.)

Personally I think paying thousands of dollars for one day of your life or going into debt for a big party like my parents did for my bat mitzvah (or both) is irresponsible. Why not use that money for a down payment on a house? Or donate it to the Trevor Project? What's the point of a wedding? Is it just a tradition that has continued on solely because people don't want to elope and break their grandparents' fragile, elderly hearts? Is it to piss off your middle school frenemy?

Though I am not personally a proponent of over-the-top weddings, I don't want to perpetuate the stereotype that it's only straight girls who go gaga over weddings. I have queer friends of all genders who are very into weddings. Possibly it's because gay people are so excited to finally be able to participate in the wedding-industrial complex that we're going overboard to have the same privileges as straight people—which honestly, I can get behind. We have so many years of seven-layer cakes to catch up on before we're "over" weddings. (And any baker who won't make a wedding cake for an

LGBTQ couple should be forced to eat a cake made by me, a person who doesn't know the difference between sugar and salt.)

————

According to *Business Insider*, the average cost of a wedding in the United States in 2018 was more than $33,000. (New York gets even more expensive, at $76,000, and New Mexico is the cheapest average, at $17,500.) Cultural affiliations can also up the cost. My friend Shradda, who had a gorgeous and large Indian wedding I attended in 2013, told me she spent $90,000 on hers, which included the dinosaur-shaped ice luge I mentioned—nontraditional for the Indian culture). When I was flummoxed by that number, she said it was cheap for an Indian wedding. In its breakdown, the Knot, a very popular wedding website, notes that the venue is the most expensive aspect, averaging $16,000 alone. Runners-up include the band ($4,000 on average) and an engagement ring ($6,000, which Allison assures me is on the low end). Two million people get married in this country every year. The wedding industry in the United States made $51 billion in 2017.

In July 2015, Vox released a video documenting a couple, Isobel and Johnny Harris, who run a DC wedding photographer business, Simple Flare. The video revealed how booking the same venue for a "family gathering" versus a "wedding" results in a price difference of $2,000. This is called "a wedding markup" or "wedding tax." Queer YouTube couple Will and RJ, in a video about planning their wedding, similarly warned that as soon as you assign the word *wedding* to anything, the price is jacked way, way up. (They tried to mitigate this by hiring a wedding planner with connections who could maybe get them discounts, but that's a gamble.)

The Vox video posits that weddings are so expensive because of asymmetric information. The idea is that with many things you purchase, you're able to guess what is too expensive and what is reasonable based on experience. Familiarity allows both buyers and sellers to agree on a fair price, which the Vox video condescendingly called "economics 101." (Okay, buddy. Chill.) But since this is most likely your first wedding, you have very little consumer experience in this area. Harris, the photographer, also admits that vendors rarely put their prices on their websites, forcing couples to inquire privately about the costs. There's very little transparency in the wedding industry. In fact, Harris said the many wedding business blogs he read when he was starting his own business all advised vendors to steer away from talking explicitly about price for as long as possible. (Shady!) He said the best thing to do is to insist on hearing a price range before any other sales pitch. "We vendors might hate it," he said in the video, "but it's the fair thing to do."

So why are so many people willing to subject themselves to an exploitative industry? The answer I got most from my friends is, "It's fun!" (Also: "You're a buzzkill, Gaby, and you always have been!") The fact is, people love their own weddings. They love other people's weddings. They love watching TV shows and movies about weddings. Society values weddings, and until that stops being the case, people will continue to want to spend on an event that is so culturally important.

If you ask me, a lot of it comes down to expensive emotional blackmail. Think of any photo you've ever seen of your great-great grandmother. It was almost certainly a wedding photo. That's the photo your ancestors will share of you—on a microchip implanted in their brains. Weddings are visual. Wedding dresses are a massive industry because of the importance our culture puts on finding the perfect dress. (For example, what are your ancestors wearing in those photos? Why does a mother cry when she sees her daughter coming out of the dressing room in that angelic white gown?)

In 2012, new bride Caitlin Kenney created a video for *Slate* magazine about the cost of wedding dresses. One of the points she made was that just because something is sold as a wedding dress, that doesn't mean it's quality. Her dress, for example, was made primarily of polyester, the same fabric as a T-shirt in an H&M that goes for thirteen bucks. When she went to an appraiser after the wedding, she guessed the fabric altogether cost $500. Kenney reveals that her dress cost her $2,730.

So what's that extra $2,230 for? Emotion? The feeling of having a fancy-ass wedding dress to take photos in and so that your friends and family will tell you you look incredible? "It's not just a dress you're paying for. It's the message you're sending," she said in the video over pretty black-and-white shots of her own wedding.

Maybe so, but you don't have to spend $2,000 on your wedding dress. You can wear a hand-me-down or rent one or buy one second-hand from places like stillwhite.com or preownedweddingdresses.com. Heck, it can be like Amy Poehler's was on *Parks and Recreation*, entirely made out of newspapers (and Leslie still had a perfect wedding to Ben!).

If you or your partner will be wearing a suit, the suit rental has to be factored in too. The Bridal Association of America estimated the cost of renting the tux at almost $200 and "groom accessories" (cufflinks, vest, shirt, tie) at $116. You may also need to pay for a fitting if you're buying a suit, or for pressing and cleaning the tux and a fee for having it overnight if you're renting. CostHelper Weddings said buying a suit could run a partner (they say *groom* but I say *partner*) anywhere from $300 to $1,500. My girlfriend works for a suit company that makes bespoke wedding suits for about $1,500 to $2,000.

I'm occasionally guilty of sentimentalizing weddings too. On Instagram, I've posted a few times a beautiful photo of my mom and dad kissing over their wedding cake. I compliment the floral crown my mom has in her hair, boasting about how flawless she looks. But more than thirty years later, her version of her wedding is less than glamorous.

In fact, when I last asked her about it, she launched into a story about how my parents originally invited 70 people, but then my father's mom, Meme, wanted to invite 125 more people at the last minute. My parents simply couldn't afford it. The bride's family usually pays for the wedding (How is that still a thing?) and my mom, with her limited resources and only one living parent, freaked out. She didn't have the money. Meme had talked my mom into buying a wedding dress that was $1,000, which is about $2,500 now with inflation. (FYI: That's above the average cost of a wedding dress in the United States, which is around $1,500 currently.) My mom insisted she could have just gone to the sale rack. The wedding kept getting more and more expensive as the things she assumed she could cut back on were deemed "necessary" for her perfect day by other people.

She said she was so stressed out that ten days before they were about to be married, she woke up in the middle of the night and told my dad she couldn't marry him. (I'd never heard this story before, by the way, so it was fun to learn that I almost didn't exist.) To ease her panic, my dad uninvited the extra 125 people the next day. (Good dude!) Still, the event was such a burden that my mom spent the whole time on Valium, which her grandmother gave to her. (Good lady!) She described her wedding day as "the worst."

WHO IS PAYING FOR THIS DOG AND PONY SHOW?

Now, when tradition is less dominant and self-expression and non-normativity are increasingly in, who's *actually* paying for all this? Is it still the bride's family? Wedding expert Anne Chertoff says it's a mix. (Of course, this is all made especially confusing if there are two brides or no brides at all.)

Most often the bride's parents cover around 40 to 50 percent of the budget, the groom's parents cover about 10 to 15 percent, and then the couple—especially these days when couples are getting married later, once they are more financially independent—pays for the rest. Of course, many couples pay for their own weddings entirely, either because they want to or because their families can't afford to foot the bill.

There's no set rule when it comes to spending for a wedding. Some people advise using a ratio to create a budget based on your income, and others suggest setting aside a savings account for it early on. Chertoff said one way to ease the financial burden is to have different family members pitch in for different things if possible. Maybe a grandmother wants to buy a dress and an uncle wants to cover the cake. Other than food and venue, the two chief expenses, wedding photography is currently the fastest-growing expense due to the rise of Instagram and Pinterest.

YouTubers Will and RJ, who spent $20,000 on their nuptials, described in their video the unique wedding-planning obstacles they faced as a gay couple. They recommend being upfront with vendors about being a same-sex couple to avoid any horrible Kim Davis–like experiences. (You remember that county clerk who refused to give marriage licenses to same-sex couples? FUN!)

On the bright side, they were able to spend less because they were forced to customize, thinking critically about every expense and whether it worked for them as two grooms. Statistically, according to a 2016 study by LOGO and the Knot, seven out of ten gay couples are more likely to foot the bill for their weddings without any family support compared to one in ten straight couples. (Sadly, too many of my LGBTQ friends have had parents who opposed their relationships and did not even attend their weddings.)

That same study revealed that gay male couples are actually now on average spending more on weddings (and also honeymoons) than they ever have before. Queer men are spending on average $33,000 for their weddings while lesbian and bi women are spending $25,000, but both numbers have grown massively in percentage since marriage equality passed in the United States in 2015. This may be because the joining of two average male incomes allows bigger wedding budgets. Queer male couples' wedding spending has risen 85 percent, and for queer women couples, that number grew 56 percent. In the same time frame from, 2015 to 2017, spending went up 1 percent for cisgender straight men and 15 percent for cisgender straight women.

As a bisexual woman, I have a soft spot for queer couples who want big weddings. We want the happy memories straight people have had forever. "These people have been thinking they'll never have an opportunity to walk down that aisle or have that first dance and now they can," said Shanie McCowen, a same-sex wedding planner in destination hubs Niagara Falls and South Florida.

McCowen, who has worked on more than 200 LGBTQ weddings, told me about a gay male couple she planned a wedding for that had only four guests. They spent $20,000 and had a private chef, rented a mansion, bought expensive gifts for their guests, booked a private driver for the whole weekend, took a helicopter ride over Niagara Falls, and spent over $2,000 for the flowers for just one room of the mansion. (Let us have this, okay? John Schneider of the *Queer Money* podcast points out that "in 28 states, you can still be fired for being LGBTQ. So while you can get married to your partner in any state in the country, if you put your wedding photo on your desk, you could get fired.") If a couple wants to cut corners, though, McCowen recommends eliminating flowers or the band or photography (maybe even the cake) and just opting for a very nice dinner with friends and family to celebrate. The most important part of the big day, in her opinion, is always who shows up, especially in families where the brides' or grooms' sexualities may be contentious subjects.

My other theory about the increase in spending for gay weddings is that there are simply more of them now. In these trying Vice President Pence times, members of the LGBT community want to get married more often to ensure certain protections. A lot of McCowen's recent clients want to be married for the legal benefits and protections. Those filing a joint tax return can get deductions and also get access to the other person's retirement money, something that eluded queer couples for decades. Legally, there's the next-of-kin benefit if a partner is sick or disabled or in the hospital: you can now make decisions on their behalf and visit them. You can also sue for wrongful death and make decisions regarding your dead spouse's burial.

LGBTQ and HIV activist Cleve Jones told Terry Gross in his 2016 episode of NPR's *Fresh Air* that he (and the rest of the world) realized the importance of marriage to LGBTQ people during the AIDS crisis in the 1980s and 1990s. Many people who'd been with their partners for decades suddenly had no rights when their partners got sick. The sick partners were unable to be added to their partner's health insurance in order to get the medication (cocktail) they needed. They were not allowed to visit each other whenever they wanted in the hospital. When the sick partner died, his long-term boyfriend had no legal rights when the family came in and, as Jones put, sold the house and kicked him out. LGBTQ marriage in the 1980s and 1990s became about much more than romance or parties. "Suddenly that little piece of paper meant, you know, the difference between actual life and death," Jones told Gross.

This is dark to think about when a marriage is just starting, but for me, it's the most convincing reason for getting married.

As of this writing, I am 29 years old, and I have a new girlfriend. We're not yet talking about marriage, though I have committed her to having six dogs sometime in the future. (Queer women know how to prioritize in relationships.)

Just in case, I looked it up, and in Los Angeles, it costs $91 to go to city hall and get married. That money is for the public marriage license fee. I'll probably want a new outfit for the occasion (white suit?) and maybe a dinner party with some friends and family. I don't have a big family or a wide circle of close friends, so that's probably fifteen people at most. If I marry someone with a big family, that person is allowed to invite fifteen people too. Future spouse: Choose wisely! I'm gonna go ahead and say:

> *Money to save for my wedding:* $1,000 (But wait: How much do six dogs cost? I'm definitely going to have to reconsider this entire wedding budget. I'm gonna need more money.)

That's how I think about it now. But it's always possible that postproposal, into my thirties or forties, I could transform into a total animal and demand my white suit be Dior and my wedding take place on stage at Coachella while Chance the Rapper officiates.

HOW TO GO ON A FREE HONEYMOON (SORT OF)

I have a friend who is on her second marriage and still paying off her first wedding. This happens because couples usually underestimate the cost of their weddings (if they don't stick to a strict budget) by about $15,000 to $20,000, according to Chertoff. That's a *huge* number. So instead of taking out a loan, many people pay for their weddings on credit cards, which offer benefits for spending. (The Points Guy would love this!)

Mandi Woodruff, a finance reporter who cohosts *The Brown Ambition* podcast, paid for her entire honeymoon with credit card rewards points. She got the Chase Sapphire preferred card with the 50,000 point sign-up offer, a bonus contingent on being able to spend the allotted amount ($3,000 to $4,000) in the allotted time frame (three to four months). She knew the deposit for her chosen venue was $3,000, so she thought, "I'm actually gonna be spending this money anyway," so why not get the benefits? But, she cautions, you should do this only if you're able to pay it back in the time frame you're given. The 0 percent interest rate lasts sometimes just six or twelve months, so you want to pay it all off before the new interest charges kick in. (If something happens and you can't pay it off before interest is charged, experts recommend taking out a personal loan to pay off the high-interest rewards card. Then pay off the personal loan, which will most likely have a lower interest rate. But this should be WORST-CASE SCENARIO.)

Then it came time to use the points for their honeymoon, and what helped was she and her fiancé were flexible about their plans. They just wanted it to be totally paid for by points. Many cards partner only with certain airlines, so she knew she had to fly United because of its partnership with Chase. They looked at the various points deals with different cities: Paris, Mykonos, Rome.

With United, "if you're doing a round trip international flight using points, you can book a free extended layover in another international city." An extended layover meant she and her fiancé could visit another city for free, so they flew from New York to Rome and then from Florence to Barcelona. The second flight was paid for by points. "In the end we ended up spending only $200 in taxes and fees for two round-trip flights to three cities, which was frigging awesome," she said.

So why doesn't everyone do this? Because it's intimidating, and there are huge risks. But if you're going to put your wedding on your credit card, be smart about it: do the math, get only what you can afford, and pick a card with benefits that will actually benefit you.

TAKEAWAYS

- If you're planning a wedding, start with an open conversation with your family and your partner's family about who can/wants to/will pay for what before it gets too out of control.

- Set a budget and stick to it.
- Look at what pieces of your wedding you can get a friend to do for cheap or as a wedding gift. Do you have a friend who bakes? Ask that person to make your cake or other treats for the reception, and you can offer to pay for ingredients. Have a friend who is killer at making playlists? That's your DJ!
- You don't need all the frills to get the benefits of marriage, but if you want frills, you do you! Weddings are built up in our culture, and it makes sense to want to go all out for something you've looked forward to and/ or feel you've earned. Just make sure you know what you're getting into down to the nitty-gritty, and leave room for unforeseen expenses.
- Consider some credit cards rewards tricks but be super careful: Wedding planning is a credit black hole.

13

DOCTOR WHO?

I have big-ass teeth, and over the past two decades, my gums had been receding. Whenever I used to eat anything particularly hot or cold, they would sting something awful. The only solution for this was gum graft surgery. So in mid-December 2015, with a full-time job and a good insurance plan, I finally got it done. But even with insurance, this procedure cost me approximately $7,000 (!), money I didn't have or expect to have anytime soon. After losing my shit over the bill, I signed up for a medical debt service called CareCredit that allowed me to pay $50 a month, which at the time I assumed I'd continue doing until I died. But, hey, at least I could eat soup without crying.

In January 2017, NPR reported on a study by the Federal Consumer Financial Protection Bureau that found that more than half the people contacted by debt collectors said it was "for medical services."

Although it's a serious problem that merits discussion, medical debt feels like fodder for old-person dinner conversation once you've run out of small talk about PBS or NPR's programming. It's also inherently shameful. There's an amazing Web comic by artist Sarah Winifred Searle about her experience going into medical debt because she was ashamed to tell her parents about needing money to pay for HPV treatments. But even if the problem isn't genital-based, it's hard to admit you're going into debt over a medical issue.

My friend the comedian H. Alan Scott is outspoken about this part of his life. Scott was diagnosed with testicular cancer a week after his 30th birthday. When he was diagnosed, he was living in NYC and had a full-time job doing social media for an event planning company. Luckily, he had insurance through his job, which he'd used only a couple of times to see a dentist. But as he found out the hard way, insurance doesn't cover everything. He is now in remission, with about $80,000 in medical debt. Scott said he doesn't answer the phone if he doesn't recognize the number (to avoid debt collectors). His "plan" for paying it off involves getting some sort of windfall in the future or dying with his debt—much like our friends with the high student loans from earlier chapters. Student debt is trending in our national conversation, but medical debt affects everyone, even those who don't have the privilege of attending college or graduate school.

Like student debt, though, Scott said people still believe his medical debt is his fault, that he's some sort of lazy person living off the state or, worse, that he gave himself cancer with poor habits. (Scott was running marathons when he was diagnosed, not that he should have to defend himself.)

Scott may have had insurance, but not all cancer-related needs are covered by insurance. For example, the biggest side effect of Scott's chemo treatments was the loss of his teeth, but dental work to fix them wasn't covered.

There was one incident where one of his teeth needed to be removed and the dentist told Scott, "We don't have time to do the implant and replacement," because he wouldn't heal in time for his chemo appointment. He could either delay chemo and have the tooth worked on and thus saved, or have the tooth pulled out completely and do the chemo. Not a great set of choices there. That's when he learned that a lot of the cosmetic surgery we need on our teeth isn't covered by insurance. "Because you don't need teeth to survive," he said. I would argue you do need teeth to survive, but apparently insurance companies think you can live the rest of your life drinking through a straw. "A lot of people just go without teeth," he said. Most of Scott's teeth are now fake and expensive.

Later in his treatments, he faced a scarier medical choose-your-own-adventure. At one point during chemo, his white blood cell count dropped low, and his body was increasingly susceptible to potentially fatal disease or infection. A decision needed to be made: Should Scott take a pause from chemo to get his white blood cell count back up, even though that would leave him vulnerable to more tumor growth? It seemed like a no-win until his doctor mentioned The Shot.

The shot, Neulasta, would increase his white blood cell

count without Scott having to go off chemo. When you google Neulasta, comment threads of cancer patients bemoan the cost of it as anywhere from $6,000 to $9,000. Scott said he remembers his costing $12,000. "Your doctor could make the case for you to have this shot, which my doctor of course did, but it's up to the insurance company to say yes or no." His insurance company said no. Scott had to choose: pay or likely die. It seems like a real version of the *Purge* films, a series of dystopian horror thrillers that I love. In the *Purge* universe, citizens of a future America are given twelve hours of one day a year to commit any crime they want without repercussions. All the people who die in the *Purge* are those who can't afford the protections—like my friend Scott. If you're wealthy, you live; if you're not wealthy, you die. The scariest part of this dystopia is how similar it is to our present day.

Scott got the shot, and he got better.

After beating cancer, and now in "insurmountable debt," he went back to his day job to pay for his treatments and daily essentials. The short-term disability payments offered by his company were running out. Four months later, he broke down in a panic. "It was just way too much to take on all at once," he said.

———

One current trend is crowdfunding your medical expenses. What was once for donors to support the arts has been co-opted for a really smart, really dark purpose.

When YouTuber Akilah Hughes was diagnosed with

huge (ultimately benign) liver tumors that had to be taken out, she turned to the Internet for help. The tumors were unexpected, and for a long time, they had gone undiagnosed. Hughes became sick and unable to work and didn't know why. She'd also accidentally let her insurance lapse and didn't realize that until she was already in need of dire medical care. When she found out she needed an expensive surgery, she turned to GoFundMe. It sounds like an episode of *Black Mirror* in which a popular Internet personality has to prove just how beloved she really is by asking her fans to literally save her life.

There's not a lot of hope for health care to get better under our current government, but it's also never been that great. The Affordable Care Act (ACA or Obamacare) was certainly helpful. In both 2014 and 2017, the *New York Times* did rundowns of how the ACA was working and found that more people were insured under it. You can find countless stories online about people who benefited, and even lived, specifically because of the ACA. Scott is able to have health insurance now only because of it; otherwise his cancer would've been considered a preexisting condition that precluded him from getting insurance. But even with insurance, unexpected medical expenses can create lifelong debt.

In an article for *Jacobin* magazine, "Ending the Empathy Gap," writer Clio Chang argues that if we decide that only certain people deserve government benefits like health care (or welfare or even schooling), then we've lost the meaning behind coexisting in a society.

The point is that everyone should get benefits—not just

the people we like or think deserve them—and that's what's so scary about crowdfunding medical expenses. You have to prove you're likable in order to live. Clio's argument is that morality, work ethic, and fan base should not decide who lives and who dies. We are not in the Hunger Games.

It's happening, though. Reporter Anne Helen Peterson wrote an incredible piece for *Buzzfeed News*, "The Real Peril of Crowdfunding Health Care," which profiled ill people who have to curate a brand on sites like GoFundMe or YouCaring to stay alive. So if you do get sick, you better also be good at marketing.

As Peterson writes about one of her subjects, "And while her story is tragic, when she first posted it, it wasn't dramatic enough to go viral on crowdfunding sites filled with similar pleas for help. She's young, but she's not an adorable child; she's extremely sick, but not with a disease that most people understand. Which isn't to suggest that her story, or her life, isn't worthy. But her situation highlights many of the under-lying issues with a new-found reliance on crowdfunding as a social safety net."

We used to be able to rely on our government for these basic public needs, but now? Nope. I donate to a website that helps teachers buy supplies for their classrooms. I gave with one click so my friend's sister could see a lung cancer specialist in Florida. You need friends, a social-media-savvy niece, or a marketing strategy for the things you used to pay taxes to ensure. It's embarrassing to have to launch a GoFundMe for health care—both for the sick person and for our society.

WHAT IF YOU *DON'T* HAVE INSURANCE?

(This is a modification of an article I posted to Thought Catalog *in 2013.)*

When I was in the ninth grade, my dad lost his job, and we lost our health insurance. That's when I started using my high school science teacher, Mr. K, as my primary health care provider.

"Mr. K," I'd say, poking my head into his lab, "let's say I had some pain on the left side of my stomach right here. Would that be my kidney, and also what can I do to make it not hurt?"

"Mr. K, hey!" I'd say, my face pressed against the glass window of the teacher's lounge. "If I have this weird bump on my knee and it hurts, should I just ice it or do I have knee cancer? Also, is knee cancer a thing you can have?"

"Gaby," he'd always reply, exasperated. "I am not a doctor. I can't legally diagnose you."

"Right. But like, my ear is kind of ringing, and what if I have scurvy?"

My time being "treated" by Mr. K showed me that you can be resourceful about health care. Here are some ways to do that—and let me know if you want Mr. K's home number. I have no boundaries.

USE GROUPON-TYPE SITES TO SEE A DENTIST OR DERMATOLOGIST OR OTHER SPECIALIST

The same websites that offer discounted massages and half-off gym memberships can also get you cheap dentist appointments (and sometimes other medical care). The only problem with these Groupon-type deals is they can be a way for the doctors' offices to get you in and then milk you for more procedures. I checked over and over again that everything they were doing was covered by the coupon. It cost $60 for a teeth cleaning. (Usually without insurance, a teeth cleaning is anywhere from $80 to $200.) The dentist tried to talk me into multiple other procedures, for $500 or more. Don't let them get you. Get in, get what's on the coupon, and get out.

FIND A THERAPIST ON A SLIDING SCALE

It's extremely messed up that treatment and preventive care for most physical ailments is covered if you have insurance, but many necessary mental health treatments are not. While needing to get mental health treatment on the cheap sucks, it's also supremely unfair that even those *with* insurance might need this bit of advice: Some therapists allow you to pay according to your income. When I lived New York, I saw someone for ninety minutes for $80 or sixty minutes for $40. (I always chose the sixty-minute option.)

Sometimes I could see them for nothing at all if I'd had a particularly rough week. My therapist was a psychology student working toward the hours she needed to graduate. I assumed paying less for therapy meant the care wouldn't be as good, but that's not true. You can also find psychiatrists on a sliding scale, but most friends I spoke to said they see one within their insurance network. Even your in-network providers may suddenly become out-of-network. This has happened to me a few times, requiring me to start over with another doctor, which can be stressful and make you feel vulnerable.

My current talk therapist in LA allows exemptions and discounts, though she's not on my insurance plan, because she trusts me and because I asked. There's no shame in asking if money is tight.

SEEK ADDICTION TREATMENT ONLINE

Alcoholics Anonymous and AlAnon meetings are free to attend, as are other recovery meetings. For online addiction recovery, there's a free site called In the Rooms. It's like Facebook for addicts and alcoholics and has a video chat feature for free online AA and NA (Narcotics Anonymous) meetings. The site's been a big help for my dad and his friends who can't afford rehab or medical services. It's not a replacement for more comprehensive recovery, but it helps when there's no other option.

TAKE ADVANTAGE OF PLANNED PARENTHOOD OR A FREE CLINIC IN YOUR AREA

If you are lucky enough to live in an area where you have access to Planned Parenthood or a similar clinic, it can be a godsend for people without health insurance. They most likely offer sliding scale services.

Of course, going on birth control (the main reason I visited PP) can be pricey. My pill, Ortho-tri Cyclen Lo, cost me $110 a pack without insurance. With insurance, it was only around $15. While I was without insurance, I went a full year without birth control pills. This meant a year of feeling *just lovely* once a month, because I didn't have a spare $110 for the pills. The only health care shortcut I tried was going on a more generic, less expensive pill, but my uterus is a fickle beast and wanted only that sweet, sweet OTC-Lo. If yours is more resilient, give another lower-cost pill a try. (Also look into the PP Pink Card, which gives you free services and significant discounts.)

THE PRICE OF BABY MAKING

This book isn't going to break the news that having a baby is expensive. But even the expensive stuff can be surprisingly *expensive.*

This may come as a shock to long-time fans of my "wild girl" brand, but I want to have a kid someday. I love babies. I beeline to any baby in the room, and I don't mean to brag, but babies love me back. (Allison's toddler niece, Bella, told her mom that I'm also her aunt. Best compliment ever.) I like the idea of teaching a little human about the world. I also know that in the next five to seven years, before I'm considered by some to be a geriatric pregnancy (GROAN), I might not be able to afford it.

Still, if being able to afford a baby was a prerequisite for having one, many of us wouldn't be here, myself included. Since my partner and I are both cisgender women, we will probably have a journey toward having a child that includes either adoption or IVF. (All options are expensive, but we'll get to that later.)

The semi-anonymous millennial authors of the blog *Bitches Get Riches*, who go by the nicknames Piggy and Kitty, told me they've both decided to remain child free to consciously ease their lifetime financial woes. They don't want to spend beyond their means and then treat their kids like their retirement plan. (My mom has joked throughout my life about me being her retirement plan. Cool.)

The money that might go toward a child's college fund or even a good preschool will go toward Kitty and Piggy's own lives, careers, and retirement funds. It's dystopian to have a system that makes people choose between having a child and securing their own futures, but here we are.

"How are you supposed to pay off your student loans and save for retirement if you're also paying for your parents' retirement?" Piggy asked. Never mind adding in a new baby. This, most likely, will be my situation soon. This idea of forgoing having children to unburden the future is common among people my age.

In fact, according to a study by the Centers for Disease Control and Prevention, the birthrate between 2007 and 2016 "fell by 338,000 [babies]." (Even something as adorable as babies seems terrifying when you picture 338,000 of them.) A Wharton School of Business study "found more than half (58%) of millennial female undergraduates do not plan to have children" and "even millennials who do want children say they do not see a clear path toward it."

New mom Anna Sale, the host of the podcast *Death, Sex & Money*, told me that as soon as she found out she was pregnant, she confirmed that her insurance covered prenatal care. It did. What she didn't know until it was too late was that it *did not* cover ultrasounds, blood work, anatomy scans, or anything else related to the pregnancy. Surprise! It's a . . . medical bill!

Indeed, babies are made up of little bills: prebirth tests

and scans, a $200 car seat, top-of-the-line breast pump equipment. The list is never-ending. Later in her pregnancy, Sale said that when the bills kept piling up, she had to start discerning whether certain tests and scans were mandatory so she could choose which were worth the cost.

There is also a ton of judgments online and IRL about what products you allow near your child. She says the various baby blogs essentially say, "If you want the really nice baby stuff, here's this list. If you want the kinda nice stuff, here's this list. And if you're on a superbudget and a bad parent, get the cheap stuff." Basically, the message is: "How much do you value your kid's life, lady???"

There's also judgment from society and other parents about going back to work after parental leave, even though most parents have to, and not every place of work even has paid parental leave. "It sucks," she said in summary. I agree.

When it's two women or two men (or two nonbinary people, depending) having a baby, there are additional costs to consider. A fan of my podcast recently wrote me an email with concerns about whether she and her wife were able to afford a baby, a dilemma I've been thinking a lot about.

As the fan wrote in this email: "Insurance will cover IVF for females in Hetero [sic] relationships if it is seen that they are having conceiving issues. However, they will not cover these service if it is a same sex couple cause it is not seen a medical issue. There is also the cost of finding a respectable sperm bank. Adoption is another option but costs a ridiculous amount of money. Others might have to turn to surrogacy to have kids." These are all expenses that come into play before the fetus is even conceived.

Sale said there's a lot of attention on (and gifts for) getting pregnant, during pregnancy, and the first year of a baby's life, but less so on helping mothers who have children older than 1 year old. People stop helping you out, she said, but the costs keep coming and only get higher as the child ages.

THE PRICE OF *NOT* BABY MAKING

So the priority is on the birth, and not on the life of the child. Sound familiar? The cost of raising a child ties directly into the abortion debate. Having and raising a baby requires resources and money not everyone has access to. Birth control of any kind costs money too, and it's also not 100 percent effective. In 2016, the *Atlantic* ran an article, "The Secret Shame of Middle Class Americans," revealing that 47 percent of Americans could not come up with $400 in the case of an emergency. An abortion can cost anywhere from $300 to $1,000, depending on when in the pregnancy it occurs. The DC Abortion Fund website says, "The cost of a first-trimester abortion can be more than a family on public assistance receives in a month." How can you pay for either a child or an abortion?

There are some abortion financial resources out there. Noel Leon works for the DC Abortion Fund, which provides money for people looking to get abortions. Before talking to Noel, I had no idea about the existence of abortion funds—nonprofit organizations that provide grants for those (largely low-income) people who need small amounts of money to pay for abortions. People call, tell the fund how much they believe they can cover and how much they need, and they are granted the money if they are eligible. There are funds like this all over the country. "To date, we have never turned away a single person who was eligible for DCAF funding," the DC Abortion Fund said on its website.

DCAF fundraises all the time, but because of limited resources, it can't afford to always meet a patient's full need. Sometimes, Noel said, the volunteers give callers suggestions like asking ten friends for $20. That's $200 extra. This is very idealistic, in my opinion, to assume that someone has ten friends with money to spare or that there are ten people they'd trust with their private medical information.

Noel said people are often terrified when calling the fund and apologize profusely for asking for money. They feel ashamed of needing an abortion and of needing financial assistance to do so, though that's the fund's job. The stigma runs deep.

When people call, Noel asks them their income, their job situation, what insurance they have, how many people live in their home, and some other questions. At first she thought these questions were too personal, but then she realized that lower-income people are used to sharing this kind of information with strangers: they often have to answer what a higher-income person might consider invasive to receive government assistance. Rich people are the ones who don't want to talk about money, she theorized, but poor people do it all the time. (This is illustrated perfectly in an incredible *New York Times* article, "What the Rich Won't Tell You," which you should read right now.)

Even in places where abortion isn't harshly regulated, it

is not always accessible. Sometimes the clinic is far away and the person can't figure out how to travel there. Sometimes they can't afford the price of the procedure or the time off work. Sometimes they have other children who take up their income and time. They can hardly afford the kids they have, let alone another baby. Some of the patients younger than 26 years old are on their parents' health insurance (which may cover abortion), but they are too scared to get one using that insurance because it means their parents will find out. Some are victims of assault.

Like Sale said, everyone cares before the baby turns 1 year old and then less and less so as the child suddenly needs government-assisted child care or welfare or food stamps. Then that same baby is considered a "financial drain on society." "Pro-life" has an expiration date.

Not covering abortions like any other medical procedure or making them harder for poorer people to get is casting a moral judgment on a medical issue. (By comparison, a lung cancer patient who smoked gets the same lung transplant as a lung cancer patient who didn't.) Deciding who can and can't based on class is asking the question, "Who can afford to have sex?" Who among us waited until we were financially stable to fuck for the first time? If you did, amazing. But most people didn't and don't. And even if everyone did wait until they were financially stable to have sex, so many people who want to have sex would probably *never* have sex! This is more archaic than abstinence only. It's abstinence forever!

BABY BANKROLLING

1. **Pump for free.** You can get a free breast pump through Obamacare. And at least one appointment with a lactation consultant must be covered. Get it while it lasts.

2. **Bunk up with your baby.** The baby should sleep in your room for at least the first six months, maybe the first year, so you don't need to spend money on a baby's room (or move into a home with another bedroom) before the baby needs it.

3. **Avoid buying baby clothes.** "I have bought my baby I think two items of clothing her entire life, and the rest have been things that other people have either given us as gifts and a lot of hand-me-downs," Sale said.

4. **Plan ahead.** What's your plan for child care and babysitting? What's your plan for eventual school? Will you save for her college or other future plans? Sale said she is "paying an arm and a leg for child care" currently and is having a hard time thinking about the kid's future beyond the next few months. But it's something you *have* to do.

5. **Check your company's parental leave policies.** If you have an employee handbook or website, you can look up the leave policy ideally before you get pregnant. Some companies will pay some or all of your salary for a set number of weeks; others simply guarantee you your job when you return. Determine whether you'll be able to get by with the level of income your company will provide (if any) for the duration of your leave.

TAKEAWAYS

- If you can afford it or are able to acquire it through work, get health insurance. Yes, the provider will try to get out of paying for care you need, but it will at least lower the amount of debt you have if something serious happens.

- Always check with your insurance or doctor about whether something is covered. You don't want to be surprised by a bill you thought insurance would handle. This sucks and involves calling customer service or nit-picking your doctor's recommendations, but it is worth avoiding hundreds or thousands of dollars of surprise debt for something you could have gone without.

- Expect many, many unexpected bills at every stage of becoming a parent. Plan for them. Prepare to spend more than you'd anticipated. Babies come with all kinds of surprises. Look into the free services available to you as a new parent. There are more than you'd think!

- Vote! Vote for elected officials who support some form of universal health care and who support reproductive rights. If we've learned anything in the past few years, it's the importance of voting.

- We should be able to make our own reproductive decisions. They're intricately tied to finances, and we need to be trusted with our own bodies. Restricting abortions and birth control and who can afford to have sex maintains the economic and class status quo, and it's cruel and dehumanizing.

14

PLAN (MICHAEL) B(AY)

Financial psychologist Dr. Brad Klontz (remember him?) told me that in order to have $50,000 a year to spend during my retirement (the equivalent of a pretty average annual salary), I would need to accrue $1.5 million in the next twenty to thirty years.

Upon hearing this figure, I sputtered. The only way this could happen, I told him, was if somehow I was able to do one big action movie in my career and then never touch that money again. (On my podcast, I called it "Plan Bay" after the blockbuster filmmaker Michael Bay.) Plan A, though, would just have to be saving the old-fashioned way.

Where does the money for my current retirement account come from? I get paid infrequently in lump sums and don't have a consistent salary, so when I do get paid, I have to break it up to make it last. As I mentioned in previous chapters, I've sold some TV shows that never aired. One of those shows netted me $50,000: I put $19,000 in a savings account, used $14,000 to pay off old debts (credit card, medical, two of my three student loans), and eventually put $16,000 into something called a SEP IRA retirement account. Wow, go me! Some experts would admonish me for starting so late. Frankly, I don't like their condescending tones.

But before we go deeper into the world of retirement savings, let's take a second to remember the incredibly important fact that not everyone *can* save for retirement. Some people who work don't have anything left in their paychecks to save. Some people in marginalized communities don't often think about the future—not just because they can't imagine having enough money to stop working or because the data shows their life spans are shorter but also because the future is just not marketed to people like them.

"When you see advertisements for retirement, and planning for your future, it's typically a straight, white couple walking down the beach holding hands together," said David Auten, half of the LGBTQ finance podcast *Queer Money*, in an interview for this book. Auten and his partner, John Schneider, worked at a top financial firm with more than $1 billion in advertising budgets, none of which went to marketing to anyone other than straight white cis able-bodied people, he said.

Statistically, the LGBTQ community (except *maybe* cis white gay men) isn't targeted, Schneider said, because they don't have as much money. For example, 40 percent of homeless youth identify as LGBTQ, and trans women of color have an average income of just $10,000 a year. That's not enough capital to think about putting something away. Some people (like those with disabilities) are even punished for saving. On my podcast, disability activist Carrie Wade told me that if a disabled person has more than $2,000 in the bank, their SSI benefits can be cut. (This is horrific, outdated, and needs to be changed.) Wade also informed me that people with disabilities could also lose their benefits if they marry someone with a higher salary, one that pushes them over the $2,000 cap.

The game developer Amy Dentata tweeted in response to the *Today Show*'s financial editor, Jean Chatzky (who has been a guest on my show), alerting her to this disability cap. Chatzky had tweeted, "By the time you're 30, aim to have 1x your annual income set aside for retirement. At 40, 3x; at 50, 6x; at 60, 8x; and by retirement, 10x." Dentata took issue with retirement coming at age 70 now, much later than in previous generations, which means people need to work longer to survive due to lower pay and the rising costs of basically everything. My father is 71 years old and does not have retirement savings. (I take issue with the "by x age, you should have y" format.)

Like Wade, Dentata reminded Chatzky that disabled people have limits, explaining that the cap on the amount of income and assets a disabled person can have before losing benefits was set in the 1980s. It's never been adjusted for inflation or to reflect the increased cost of living. Basically, people on SSI are not legally allowed to save for retirement.

Meaningful retirement savings also require a level of financial knowledge and access to money that many people do not and cannot have. This all needs to be acknowledged. But for now, let's answer some basic questions you might have about retirement funds if you're looking into having one, like what's a 401(k) versus a Roth IRA or SEP IRA? (This information is partially taken from the Department of Labor's official site.)

REGARDING RETIREMENT FUNDS

401(K)

A 401(k), named after its subsection in the Internal Revenue Code, is where employees of a company choose to have a portion of their salary put into the company's 401(k) plan (made up of different investments) before taxes. In some cases, the employer matches all or some of these contributions (you should look into if your place of work does this).

There is a dollar limit on the amount an employee can contribute each year, which the federal government sets (in 2018 the limit is $18,500, so most people don't have to worry about maxing it out, unless you have an extra $18,000 in your salary you don't need). Employees can choose their own investments from the options the company provides. Your employer maintains the account.

Contributions to 401(k) are not taxed when you put the money in, but the money *is* taxed when you take it out upon retiring (or any other withdrawals). Then you could end up paying a large chunk, depending on what happens to income taxes in the next thirty or so years and how much you take out each year. This kinda sucks. Usually, though, people earn less when they're retired, so income taxes are likely to be lower than when they're working. Still sucks, though!

If you take money out of it before you retire, you pay a LOT of extra taxes on it and have to pay it back (in this case, the future you is just loaning the money to the present you). You can start taking retirement money out without penalty when you're 59½. (Weird.) And you must start taking it out when you're 70½ (also weird) unless you're still working. If you look at your paycheck, you can see the deductions if you opted into it.

When you leave a company, you can take your 401(k) with you. You just have to ask. How do you ask HR at your full-time job for your 401(k) if you're leaving the company or even if you just want to see what's in it? I was worried about saying something silly like, "Hello, I'd like my 401(k) rolled over to my new job, please." Turns out that's exactly what to say. Get a statement of your account. Log into the site to see what's happening in your 401(k). Find out what investments are in it. Find out what investment firm your company is using, and what fees it is charging to look after your money. Make sure you're not overpaying in fees on your 401(k). Fees can include plan administration fees like the costs of upkeep on the 401(k), like accounting and record keeping, or individual service fees. The biggest of the fees might be an investment fee that varies depending on the particular investments you're making in your 401(k), as well as sales and commissions fees. The information about fees can be found in your 401(k)'s breakdown, also called a prospectus. According to *Business Insider*, the long, often dense document "should lay out expenses associated with various investment options, as well as the past investment performance." You can also find this information in your company's benefits booklet, which they are required to have on hand. HumanInterest.com listed 1.37 percent of assets invested in the plan as an average fee. If you feel your fees are too high, you can look into the contents of your 401(k) and figure out other alternatives.

IRA

An individual retirement account is not tied to employment, so it's usually good for freelancers. The website The Motley Fool writes that traditional IRAs don't have income restrictions, so anyone, regardless of income, can contribute to one as a retirement plan. As with a 401(k), the contributions are tax deductible, but you have to pay taxes whenever you make withdrawals.

You can make contributions to the plan only until the age of 70½. It's a good option if you work a job that doesn't offer a 401(k) or are a freelancer, and you're going to be contributing only a few thousand dollars each year (in 2018, the limit for people under 50 is $5,500).

ROTH IRA

Unlike a 401(k) or traditional IRA, Roth IRA contributions *are* taxed, but withdrawals *are not* taxed—so you basically never have to pay taxes on the portion of the account that is return on investment (what you've earned)—just on the contributions you've made. "Since you've already paid taxes on your contributions, you are free to withdraw them (but not any investment gains) at any time without an early withdrawal penalty," according to The Motley Fool's reporting on IRAs. "For this reason, Roth IRAs can be great ways to build up an emergency fund, as well as for retirement savings."

You maintain the account yourself (or with an accountant), without an employer, so it's useful for self-employed people.

There's no age limit where you have to stop contributing or to take the money you contributed out, but you can't take out the money your investment *earns* until you've retired. The money you're *contributing* is separate from the money you're *earning* on your retirement investments in the IRA. (I know it's confusing. Read it again. I had to, and I wrote it.)

SEP IRA

This is what I have. Similar to the Roth, it's mainly used for self-employed people and business owners to act in place of an employer 401(k). The SEP and the Roth IRAs are similar, so if you're a freelancer or self-employed, do a little research on what works best for your career. According to The Motley Fool, the benefits of a SEP over a Roth are that SEP IRAs have higher contribution limits so those who have them can contribute more to their retirement. "Since contributions to a SEP are made on a pretax basis, you can get a nice tax deduction," the Fool reported.

The issue is that choosing requires a whole lot of guessing. Who among us knows what we want our life to look like in forty years? (If you do, I bow to you.) Or what our life will *be* like when we retire? This is what makes retirement planning so tough. How do you know if you'll be in a higher tax bracket when you retire? In forty years, your lifestyle could completely change. Taxes could completely change! We could all be living in space! Totally stressful and confusing!

———

Bola Sokunbi, a Nigerian financial expert who created the site CleverGirlFinance.com, told me on my podcast: "Come age 65 or whatever your age that you want to retire is, there's no one waiting for you with a bottle of champagne and a house on the beach and a million dollars saying, 'Hey! Hey, girl! I built this for you. I saved this for you.' You have to do it yourself."

Before this year, saving for retirement was not something I ever considered. I just didn't have the money, was too much in debt, and was too embarrassed to save in tiny amounts like fifty cents or a dollar. It didn't seem like it mattered. Also, my parents never taught me about it. And as I've said, financial services are not marketed to people like me.

Research shows cisgender women outlive cisgender men by almost a decade. Women may need retirement money for longer, but we don't make as much because of the wage and investment gaps. In general, men die younger than women do AND with more money. If a financial product is marketed to anyone other than cis men, it's usually not done well: "They just slap pink on it and say 'Here! Finance for women!'" Sokunbi said. (To counter this, check out Sallie Krawcheck's company Ellevest, a company created to help women specifically to invest, to combat the investment gap. Krawcheck has mocked the Wall Street symbol as being a literal bull. Not very inviting.)

In her eye-opening book, *Pound Foolish*, Helaine Olen takes a questionnaire to see how well she'd do at saving for retirement. One of the questions was a metaphor regarding college basketball, and she got it wrong. (Obviously MANY women and nonbinary people know about sports. Olen, who grew up in a time when women were not encouraged to participate in sports, just doesn't.) The test told her she'd be bad at odds and therefore bad at investing. She argued that all it proved was she didn't know anything about sports and that retirement information is primarily aimed at men (who typically might recognize sports metaphors). (Some men.) (Look. You get it.)

The only people who have access to my SEP IRA are me and my accountant, Dan. I think of any money I put in there as nonexistent. It is gone once I give it to him. If you're able, you can set it up to have some money automatically deposited into a retirement fund each month, and then you'll never think about having that money. I don't do that, but I try to put chunks of money in whenever I get paid enough. Then, I *Eternal Sunshine* it from my memory.

———

There are other income streams available for when you retire, like Social Security, for example. The average Social Security income is $16,320 a year, but that's not really enough for the average person to live comfortably on. So an American retiree, excluding Social Security and assuming the 22.5-year-figure is correct, needs 1.3 million for retirement, just like Klontz said. And this is just an estimate, which gets higher if you get sick or with any other extenuating circumstance, but even the "low" $1.3 million seems distant and impossible.

"If you don't have a million dollars in your life, how can you have a million dollars saved up as a retiree?!" I asked Sokunbi. "That seems nuts!"

"If you can save only a dollar every paycheck, save a dollar," Sokunbi said. She recalled trying to start saving money herself in a way I was too ashamed to do until recently. She had one extra dollar in her checking account that she tried to transfer to savings. It was too little money for an online transfer, so she took the one dollar and drove to the bank to deposit it without embarrassment. (Dang, girl!)

"It's not about the amount, the one dollar; it's about building the habit and the consistency of putting money aside because if you can't save when you have a little, you're not going to save when you have a lot of money," she said.

Sokunbi told me that even pennies on the street add up (I have a penny jar in my kitchen! Am I doing this right?), and once you're motivated to save, you'll make other changes, like thinking about your expenses and cutting down specifically to contribute to retirement savings. Saving needs to become second nature. Even if you save $1 a week for two years like Sokunbi used to, you have $104 that you didn't have before. The retirement system obviously isn't designed for everyone to succeed, so Sokunbi's advice is to just forget the system and do what you can individually.

"Does that mean earning more money? Does that mean cutting down on your expenses? Does that mean getting a part-time job? Does that mean starting a business? You know, going back to school to get more education for the next level you're trying to get to?" she asked. Unlike my increasingly socialist agenda (LOL), Sokunbi said she sees no point in worrying about anyone but yourself. It's very John Galt of her, and I don't love it, but maybe there's a way to meet in the middle. The system is broken, which is why, she said, you have to be proactive and protect yourself.

In 2017, CNBC reported that 41 percent of people my age had not yet started saving for retirement, mainly because of a lack of disposable income. (I didn't start saving for retirement until I was 29.) In 2017, *Fortune* reported that 70 percent of Gen Xers rely on 401(k)s and the majority of baby boomers rely on Social Security and pensions for retirement. A 2017 Center for Generational Kinetics study showed that 12 percent of Gen Z is already saving for retirement, which is much higher than millennials, who were around their age during the economic downturn in 2008.

Piggy and Kitty from *Bitches Get Riches* said people in their twenties and thirties need to stop looking at retirement as the time when we're no longer relevant to the world. I'll probably still want to write even as I age, just as I was writing stories when I was 6 years old. But like when I was a child, I won't want to have to be writing for money. (Although does anyone want to pay me for my second-grade short story about a soccer summer camp?)

"Retirement" has to be redefined to mean "working without stressing about getting paid or being beholden to needing to pay bills." "When you frame it in those terms, saving for retirement becomes saving for freedom," Kitty said. This change in definition is what motivates those millennials and Gen Z who can actually save.

And it looks like we'll need to. It's debatable whether government benefits like Social Security will exist by the time millennials and Gen Z will be able to use them. One-third of retirement-age Americans rely on the benefits. Some experts insist people my age will be able to access Social Security, and their big argument is, "Well, what other option does the government have other than to keep providing it?" (I don't know, man. Have you ever seen a science-fiction movie?)

Half of the millennials surveyed in 2014 by the Pew Research Center said they didn't believe Social Security would be around when it came time for them to retire. (The age presumption here is a staggeringly young 65 years old. This does not jibe with reality, which has people retiring way older than that.) However, in 2015, *HuffPost* reported that "with government data on tax income pointing to a continuation of about three-quarters of scheduled benefits through the end of 2089, millennials will likely receive some Social Security—just possibly not as much as Americans receive now."

"The government's official position," a *Time* article called "Will Social Security Still Exist When I Retire?" reported, "is that there is enough money saved to pay benefits at the currently scheduled amounts until 2041. The Social Security Administration admits on its website that benefits will likely be reduced after that, barring changes that improve the financial strength of the system." NerdWallet estimates it will be less by around $300.

Those who believe there will be no Social Security blame baby boomers for sucking it dry, and those who disagree think those people are being hyperbolic and alarmist.

My stance? Trust no one. If Social Security exists, great. That's an extra thousand or so dollars a month. If it doesn't, we have to be prepared some other way. Remember when we were all being told the 2016 election was a lock for the Democrats? Because I do. And who knows what a Republican administration is going to do to the funding for government benefits like Social Security? (I know what. It's to pay for golden Jet Skis for all their friends.)

INVESTING

So where else can you put your money, other than a savings account or 401(k), to ensure a somewhat stable future? Other investments! And not just the stock market but investments in the waves of the future.

In early 2018, I purchased Litecoin, a cryptocurrency similar to Bitcoin but less expensive. (Wow! These are all words!) Bitcoin, invented by an anonymous creator in 2009, is a digital currency that can be sent between anyone in the world directly from one user to another without a bank or other middleman. The price is determined the way stock prices might be, based on the currency's popularity. The *New York Times* described Bitcoin in a 2017 article, "What Is Bitcoin and How Does It Work?" saying the "system is run by a decentralized network of computers around the world keeping track of all Bitcoin transactions, similar to the way Wikipedia is maintained by a decentralized network of writers and editors."

I invested $505 in Litecoin using a digital wallet called CoinBase. I track my investment using the CoinBase app. I'm telling you this as if I understand any of it. I don't. At the time when I bought two Litecoins, Bitcoin had shot up to be worth $14,000 for one Bitcoin. (Bitcoin had had a moment a few years before, and then people largely forgot about it. Suddenly cryptocurrency was back in the limelight.)

Litecoin is my first crypto-investment. I thought it was a semi-safe place to start. Investing is like gambling. If I lose, the money is only money I am okay losing anyway. If I make even a little money, then I'll be pleasantly surprised.

Comedian Samantha Ruddy had bought Bitcoin back

when it was hot and forgot about it. She tweeted in 2018 that she checked her investment for the first time around the same time I bought Litecoin and found she'd made $700 she didn't previously know about. TechCrunch writer Taylor Hatmaker even created a Google Doc–based cryptocurrency guide specifically for queer people to encourage investing among minorities. (It's a thorough ten-page document that notes that while capitalism is bad, Hatmaker would rather minorities benefit from it if the system has to exist. Go look for her work if you're interested!)

Investing in cryptocurrency is complicated because investing in general is complicated. On my show, I interviewed Sallie Krawcheck, who survived working on Wall Street in the 1980s, a brutally hostile male environment. (She told me she often found photocopies of "male nether regions" on her desk.)

Like Hatmaker, Krawcheck advised marginalized people of all kinds who can afford to invest to start doing so. Ellevest works with stocks, which she describes very patiently for me as "ownership in a company . . . and a company's earnings." It helps a company raise money to grow the company. Here's what I learned from talking to her:

1. There are no guarantees in investing. She suggested a mutual fund that includes investments in multiple big groups of companies (referred to as a "portfolio") so your eggs aren't all in one basket.

2. Don't think of it as gambling, but rather as making an investment in the future of the American

economy. Even if you feel that you don't know any-thing, everyone is playing a game. You deserve a spot at the table if you want it.

3. Women are not, as the stereotype goes, risk averse. They are risk *aware*, Krawcheck said. (And I'm sure other marginalized people are similar.) This is not a bad thing. Get all the books or read all the credible websites so you can learn the terminol-ogy. Don't be afraid to do the research and ask the questions.

4. Look for people and companies that serve people similar to you. Krawcheck said a lot of investing advice for women is gendered and cutesy, citing, "Don't buy shoes, ladies! Invest!" (This is why she created Ellevest.) Get your money advice from people who can relate to you on your level. There are, for example, not that many LGBTQ financial advisers, but one I spoke to, Natalie Miller, is one of the first out trans financial advisers in the coun-try. Times are changing!

5. Even if you are a cis woman with a cis male part-ner, don't let him take the reins on your money or investments because you don't want to be both-ered or to lean on average gendered stereotypes. Krawcheck said retirement homes are 80 percent single women. You have to learn this on your own.

6. Start now. Even if you don't have that much, Krawcheck said, most women who have paid off debt should be investing 10 percent of their salary instead of only gaining small interest in a stagnant savings account.

Obviously this advice applies to only a certain subset of women who want to invest and are able to do so. And while investing can certainly help you and is a way for women to work within the system, it's a system that tends to favor middle- and upper-class women (and other types of minorities in that same socioeconomic class). As we get to in Chapter 16, "The System," I'm on the fence as to if the solution lies in making the most you can by participating in a system that has largely excluded us or by working to dismantle that system for everyone. Maybe it's a little of both.

EXPENSES TO PLAN FOR AFTER YOU RETIRE

1. **Housing.** Do you own your home, or do you rent? What area do you want to live in? Planning for retirement is very different in San Francisco or New York than it is in Missoula, Montana, or Lake Havasu, Arizona. You may be able to get a bigger place for less money or for less rent elsewhere.

2. **Transportation.** How are you going to get around? Can you walk most places? Does a ride-sharing service exist in your city if you can no longer drive? If you have a car, you'll have to factor car payments (insurance, gas, maintenance) and possibly auto loan payments into what you'll need for retirement.

3. **Food.** OBVIOUSLY. You'll still need to eat in retirement.

4. **Health Care.** This can be hardest to plan ahead for. Colon cancer runs in my family. It's why my mom started getting colonoscopies waaay before the recommended time. So I know that colon cancer is something I should look out for. Does that mean I should put aside some extra money in case I get colon cancer? In an ideal world, sure. You never know what could happen to you as you age. Keeping that in mind when saving, while not being terrified of the inevitability of death, is a good idea. (Keeping it light over here.)

5. **Entertainment.** On a happier note, you also need to save for having fun! You'll still want to go to the movies or buy records or attend museum exhibits or play virtual reality bridge or whatever other activities we'll all be doing when we retire. You need to be able to enjoy your life.

TAKEAWAYS

- It's super hard to plan for retirement when you need or want money for things RIGHT NOW. But getting in the habit of putting even a little away regularly, if you're able, can help avoid bigger, scarier problems when you are older.

- For many marginalized people, participating in the system (e.g., investing, saving) is a way to ensure their futures. But it can also feel like you're benefiting while others stay in poverty. Try to find a balance between doing what you can for yourself and taking political action, volunteering, marching, or voting to create a better system.

- Retirement doesn't mean becoming useless to society. It means doing only work you want to do or work you don't need to get paid for.

- You have permission to get Starbucks or a manicure or new sneakers, or whatever your indulgence is. We COULD all be blown up next week, and you're allowed to enjoy life now even if you don't make a lot of money. But don't rely on the end of the world or on someone else, because you could end up living a very long time. (Maybe we'll all be immortal brains in jars. Who can say?)

15

WHERE THERE'S A WILL, THERE'S A WAY

When we were little, my sister and I would play a very morbid game called "Writing Your Will." The game was that we'd sit down and write on a piece of computer paper what we'd leave to whom if we passed away. Then we'd compare notes and argue about what we wanted. Why wouldn't she leave me her Gameboy? Why wouldn't I leave her my Pokemon cards? What favors could I do to get more stuff in her will? What was she leaving my parents versus what I'd chosen to leave them? Whose inheritance to our extended family was nicer? We also knew these weren't *real* wills—or so we thought.

Turns out, according to estate lawyer David Shapiro, that if a will is written in the dead person's own handwriting, it could be legally binding—even if it's on a piece of computer paper and drafted in crayon. (He also said some states are now allowing text messages to count as wills. What emojis will you use in your wills, guys?)

Wills are complicated, and trusts, which are supposed to eliminate some of the hassle, can also be complicated because, of course, *families* are complicated. You're banking on there being even one reasonable responsible person in charge after a death. (In my own family, we're all relying on my hippie aunt because the pickings are slim, y'all.)

The way my family is set up, I never assumed I was getting an inheritance. When I hear the word *inheritance*, I think about some douchebag at a boarding school in Connecticut telling his potential girlfriend that he's all set once his trust fund kicks in. Or some other douchebag complaining about struggling to get a start-up off the ground even though all the seed money came from their parents. Or maybe the beginning of a movie where douchebag Adam Sandler has to go back to school in order to inherit his father's company. I clearly know a lot about inheritances (and douchebags). I was pretty sure all I'd inherit was debt and some Native American art. (It's lovely, but my parents really gotta cut out buying dreamcatchers and turquoise. My childhood home is an ode to appropriation at this point.)

So here's the big Dunn family inheritance problem: When Pepe died, my grandmother was left $2 million liquid. Over the next five years, she blew through half of that. What did Meme spend $1 million on? "Stuff," my dad said in 2017. Makeup, rings, dresses, scarves, anti-aging creams. The twisted part is the longer she lives, the more time she has to spend that money, the less inheritance my dad and his sister get. And Meme, by her own admission, doesn't care.

What may seem cruel in print is just Meme's way. Because

of what she went through during the war, our family right-fully cuts her a lot of slack on her enjoyment of life. Some-times she says things that make you want to snuggle her, and then two seconds later, she says something else that makes you want to strangle her. She seems to be delighting in how tense her spending has made everyone. She's in charge now.

Luckily, my aunt and my dad are best friends. They've worked it out so that whatever inheritance they get, they split up in a way that makes sense, regardless of what Meme has put in her will. (No one narc to Meme! I'm trusting you guys.)

My sister, my brother, and I have our shares cut out for us, but I can't get a real number out of either Meme or my father. I probably won't until it comes time to actually han-dle her affairs. My brother has a wife and a kid. My sister and I are currently unmarried and both childless. I'd assume my brother and his family are getting more money. That just seems fair, but I'm only guessing.

Pepe wasn't a money factory to me; he was a human being who called me and my friends "good-looking tomatoes" and danced with me and my sister by letting us stand on his feet. He kept Snickers bars in the freezer because he liked to eat them that way as dessert, and he always seemed to be wearing a dif-ferent very comfy sweater over a button-down shirt. I don't ever remember thinking, when we were at Pepe's funeral or even in the five years afterward, about what his money meant for us.

I used to ask my mom all the time when I was a kid: What would happen to us if she and my dad died? (Sensing a morbid theme here?) I believe the game plan was for me to go live with my dad's sister and her husband, which worked for me. Their house was sweet, with its lush garden and big fish tank. I was down to move in, worst-case scenario. But now that I'm an adult, am I financially prepared in case my parents die?

Both of writer Eden Dranger's parents had passed away by the time she was in her early 20s. Her mother died first, and the funeral, she remembered, was expensive because her family wanted her mom buried in Israel. She had to fly there with her mother's dead body in storage underneath the plane. Even more terrifying than that nightmare was that her mother didn't leave a will, and to this day it's why Eden and her sister don't speak anymore. They fought over terms. Death without established guidelines, as Shapiro said, causes a lot of family strife.

"At the end, it's kind of sad that money is what we're all mad about," Eden said.

No one wants to talk about money—and they especially don't want to talk about death. That's why, Eden said, her mom didn't leave a will, which is basically a hybrid of the two. But by not thinking or talking about either, she warned, you're doing your family members a huge disservice.

You would think after the mess with her mother, her family would have learned, but it happened again when her father died. Eden was 24 when she found out he hadn't left a will either! Four weeks before he died of brain cancer, Eden said she quickly got a lawyer on the advice of a friend, and she had her father put together a trust for her. During the whole process, she was stressed about the future and grieving her father's imminent death—a surreal combination of emotions she recommended other people avoid.

She started worrying about the estate going to probate court. Probate, according to LegalZoom, is "the legal process through which a deceased person's estate is properly distributed to heirs and designated beneficiaries and any debt owed to creditors is paid off." This tends to happen when people don't have a clear, valid will or only their own name on their assets and no will.

"The probate process can be long and costly, taking months and sometimes years to resolve. The longer it takes, the more it will cost, leaving potential heirs with less than the deceased may have intended," FindLaw.com advises. Without the trust, Eden would have had to hire a probate lawyer (which she couldn't afford) to help her get access to her father's assets.

So as a new orphan, Eden had to immediately jump into action to avoid probate and figure out what to do with everything her parents had accrued during their lives. Death certificate in hand, she headed to Bank of America to get access to her father's bank account. She was surprised to learn it was overdrawn by $2,000. His brain cancer had caused him to buy all kinds of unnecessary products in bulk from Costco. He'd also stopped paying his bills or paying attention to his bills, some of which were set on automatic payment, so car payments, insurance payments, and mortgage payments were all going through. He'd also stopped paying his credit card bills.

Eden couldn't afford to deal with all of this. Luckily, her mom's money had been left in a bank in Israel. She transferred that to her account in LA and used it to pay for her dad's mistakes and his funeral. Before that, Eden said, she had maybe

$1,000 to her name. For his burial, she chose the "IKEA of funerals," as she called it— the cheapest options all around— which still ran her $10,000. (Traditional Judaism doesn't allow for cremation, the truly cheapest option. USfunerals.com says a cremation runs $1,500 to $3,000 on average. But Eden's extended family was pressuring her to follow Jewish law.)

Buying a plot in the ground is essentially buying real estate. Eden joked that a great gift you can give your family would be buying a burial plot for yourself in advance. She called the plots "the biggest scam" next to funerals. "I was pretty shocked that they demand so much money. It's like, 'They're dead! They're not going to even appreciate this!'" she said. I'm inclined to agree. Whenever someone tells me that because of my tattoos I won't be able to be buried in a Jewish cemetery, I always reply, "I'll be dead, so who cares?"

When TV writer Steve Basilone's mom died of cancer, Steve was her only child, so most of the responsibilities fell on his shoulders. He remembered, in the wake of her death, being on hold with the bank and then waiting in endless lines. He only sort of knew beforehand that he was the executor of her estate, because when she got sick, Steve didn't want to spend her last months talking about what he'd do without her. He said he regrets it now, but part of him felt that it was the job of the person who was dying to bring it up. He also understands that accepting that you're dying is a huge emotional journey so he wants to cut his mother some slack. (Super fair.)

On top of grieving his loss when she passed, he felt kicked while he was down by all the bureaucracy and minutia. Her funeral, which cost nearly $12,000, required flowers, an urn, printed photos of her to use, a card with a quote, and many other choices. (None of this was specified in her will. It's just what Steve wanted to do to celebrate her.) For a wedding, you spend a year and a half planning a fun party, but after someone dies, Steve said, "You're spending two days while you're sad as shit planning a very, very sad party."

Paying off his mother's debts cost him $30,000 to $35,000. "I guess I thought before this, a lot of little bills would just go away— like, 'Oh, they died; that's sad. You get a pass.'" This was not the case. "A bunch of little bullshit bills," he called them. His mother had American Express points that he just let go. It was too much trouble to get a death certificate and prove that he was the executor. He could also get them only in gift cards. "It was just like the most ridiculous thing, and it was at the tail end, and I was just like, fuck it, I don't care. I just don't."

Eden inherited her parents' house—her childhood home, where she still lives today. She pays the mortgage on it. When I went there to tape a podcast in 2016, she was still surrounded by their things: closets of their clothes, their art hanging on the walls, their furniture in the living room. Part of her wants to do something with all of it, but part of her still feels too overwhelmed.

Writer Rob Penty wrote in a *Billfold* article, "What I Learned about Money after My Parents Died," about inheriting a home and money from his parents, who passed away within six months of each other. Penty said everyone expected him to have become an heir to a fortune. (His roommate immediately asked if they could get a new TV.)

Instead, he was left, like Eden, with a house with two

mortgages on it and some debts. Much of his money went into escrow at first, which means it was being held by a third party as a midway point. Penty had a lawyer help him figure out some of his English father's dental bills. People he expected to be understanding were not. His father's dentist of thirty years immediately demanded her money in full without apology, even though she'd been a family friend. (He'd tried to work out a payment plan with her office.) That's when Penty realized no one was going to play nice just because he was now an orphan.

PREPARING (FINANCIALLY) FOR DEATH

It's not fun to think about, but we're all going to lose our parents or guardians someday, if we haven't already. For when that happens, here are some things to know:

- You might not have to pay their hospital bills. This one blew me away. Not paying them back gives your dead parents (or loved one) a bad credit score, but as Eden said, "Who cares? They're dead." Be careful though: commonwealth.com reported that many states have "filial responsibility" statutes that sometimes hold adult children responsible for a deceased parent's medical debt. Make sure you know what the laws are in your state.
- You don't have to pay back their credit card debt unless you cosigned on the card. Eden's dad had a credit card balance of $30,000. She told the com-

pany her dad had died, and she was unemployed. All she could afford to pay was $5,000. The company said "okay." "I was so mad that I didn't ask for less!" she said. "They know that most of the time, they just don't get anything."

- If you're inheriting a positive amount after debts have been settled and the funeral has been paid for, think carefully for at least six months about where that money should go. Penty says that's how long you need to grieve before you can make a level-headed decision. In his piece for *Billfold*, he wrote that he invested the money in buying a home in Brooklyn "that is roughly one-eighth the size and double the price of my childhood home." (New York, city of dreams!) If you inherit your parents' house and you don't want to live there immediately (like Eden does), you should sell it. Penty felt awful selling his childhood home, but realistically, he had to consider the upkeep of a house that large and the cost of property taxes.

- It's best not to have siblings. In an interview for this book, Penty said he was lucky to be the sole executor of the will. His parents didn't have a fortune to begin with, and he didn't have to split any of it with anyone else or run anything by a sibling before he did it. "No family drama," he said. (Jesus Christ, what is that like?)

- Be prepared for mountains of paperwork. Penty compared it to applying to college: "It's just a bunch of paperwork and it takes months. You can't rush it even if you try. Sit down and get through all the paperwork, and pay attention even if the words make your eyes cross."

GETTING YOUR OWN MORTAL SHIT IN ORDER

What about if *you* die young? I'm 29. It feels like it's not an option. But then I think about my friend's father, whose wife died at 31, leaving him with two young daughters. She didn't have a will or life insurance, which, he said, left a lot of confusion for their family. How could she have known she'd pass away so young? I can't know either.

Lawyer David Shapiro said if you're that young, you probably don't have assets other than your bank account or maybe a car. In that case, he said, name someone as a beneficiary to avoid ambiguity. Maybe a lot of us don't have assets, but some young people do own homes. I don't, but I do have a retirement account. At the end of 2017, my accountant, Dan, asked me for a name to put on my retirement account as a beneficiary in case I die. I hadn't thought about it. I chose my mother for no reason other than I trust her to figure it out. When I told her, she said, "Let's hope I never have to."

What about if, like my friend's mother did, you have people depending on you for financial help? What happens to them when you die? And, Shapiro added, what if you have a favorite niece you want to give a specific gift to? Or just something with immense sentimental value that you hope goes to your brother? Shapiro said if those are the case, a will is a good idea for anyone at any age.

Common advice says to create a will when you have children, but if you don't plan on having children, it should be when you have significant assets. I don't specifically have a will (my only non-monetary asset is my very banged-up Toyota Prius), but I've told my mom (and, in the worst case, where my mom and I are both dead, my sister) to divvy everything up as she sees fit. It's a weird discussion to have.

When I was home for Thanksgiving in 2017, we talked about how my little sister has power of attorney (even though she's the youngest sibling). POA means my parents have given her "written authorization to represent or act on another's behalf in private affairs, business, or some other legal matter," according to Wikipedia. I don't mind. My sister has said she'd be okay making the hard decisions if both of my parents were too injured to do so. My mom expressed to us over breakfast that she wants us to give her an "ecologically friendly" funeral. (She's worried about Earth running out of burial space, and also it's less expensive.)

My mom's mom and my dad's stepdad have physical grave sites that we visit every so often, but I've stopped feeling an emotional connection to the spots. It's like the Mary Elizabeth Frye poem "Do not stand at my grave and weep / I am not there I do not sleep." My mom agreed with me.

A few years ago, she asked me what I'd want her to do if I died beyond donating my organs to help others. (That's just my wish. I know it freaks some people out.) I told her to guess what I'd want. She said I'd want to be cremated and then have the ashes sprinkled on the lawns of my enemies. What a cheap option!

TAKEAWAYS

- Have these hard conversations. Sort out your family's and your own financial shit before you're dealing with possible trauma and grief. Making long-lasting money decisions during an emotional time is not ideal. The more you have planned out, the less likely you are to cause deep familial resentments or make rash choices people are unhappy with.

- If there is a risk of your losing a family member anytime soon, research exactly what you'll have to take care of after that person dies and what you can leave by the wayside. There's no sense in doing or paying more than you have to during this difficult time.

- Think about your own posthumous financial trail. It's something no one wants to do, but the real gift is making sure everyone is taken care of before it's too late.

16

THE SYSTEM

When I talk about "the system," I'm sure I look like Charlie from *It's Always Sunny in Philadelphia* trying to crack the case of Pepe Silvia. (Find the clip on YouTube. It's very relatable.) It's an unsolvable catch-22: How can I make sure I have what I need to exist and succeed within a broken system without supporting that system?

To borrow from my own tweet:

Me on Twitter: Burn the capitalist system
Me on Amazon: Check out my wish list

The first season of my podcast is devoted to conversations with people about their complicated relationships to money. By season 2, I was increasingly radicalized. The more I learned about money, the more of a socialist I became. But can I actually be a socialist? Do I have to move to the woods to do it?

Let's back up. Capitalism is defined as a social system where goods and services are provided by individuals based on supply and demand (with prices determined by competition). This is more or less our current system. So what then is socialism?

In 2016, the membership of the Democratic Socialists of America (DSA) went from 8,000 dues-paying members to 25,000, according to a 2017 Vox article, "9 Questions about the Democratic Socialists You Were Too Afraid to Ask." (You don't know me! You don't know what I'm afraid to ask!)

The same article attempted to explain what the DSA wants and believes in: socialism, or the abolition of capitalism and an economy run by the workers. How they plan to achieve this is hotly debated. The article continues, "According to DSA's current mission statement, the government should ensure all citizens receive adequate food, housing, health care, child care, and education."

"The incentive by the employer or the capitalist is to keep your wages low, while your incentive is to make more money because you gotta survive, and it's an antagonistic relationship," said Brandon Peyton-Carrillo, a member since 2013 and the national facilitator for the DSA Solidarity Economy Working Division. Peyton-Carrillo suggested abolishing the worker/owner relationship and allowing the workers to own companies and run them as a democracy.

Here's an example: When I lived in New York, I'd accompany friends to the Park Slope Food Co-op, a grocery store that is owned and operated by the people who shop there.

According to the Co-op's website, there are 17,000 members who take turns working at the co-op in exchange for 20 to 40 percent off their groceries. The point is to participate in your community, get more affordable food, and be able to have a vote about the goings-on at the place where you buy your groceries. This is what the DSA would want for all sorts of services.

Seems great, right? But many people think it doesn't work. In 2016, a Gallup poll revealed that 60 percent of Americans still believe in capitalism over socialism. My guess is it's because they think they'll be supporting other people who don't work as hard as they do. Overthrowing capitalism honestly sounds exhausting. Some believe socialism requires a strike. If the workers stop going to work, production halts and the rich can't make money. But then neither can the poor. And also some workers might just go to work anyway. There's no leverage.

Peyton-Carrillo said lower-income and working-class people make the mistake of thinking there's only one way to do things because that's all they've experienced, and they believe that the people at the top must deserve their wealth. They bow to knowing their role, hoping to get crumbs from the table. But, he said, people should know there's an alternative, one that has been part of society for a long time.

Knowledge is power, and knowledge, it turns out, is pissed off. There have been a few nights where I've paced in my pajamas going over how hopeless breaking the system is unless everyone gets on board—and getting everyone on board with anything political is a mess.

The capitalist system lives because of our continued participation in it. And it thrives on mocking socialists and activists as "burnouts" or unrealistic, naive dreamers. It feeds on every Facebook post by a rich baby boomer about entitled millennials asking for more from their employer. Peyton-Carrillo knows people romanticize competition instead of working together. They think, "How could I beat that other motherfucker across the table from me??" not, "How can I work with this person?"

There was a tweet that went viral in 2017 about a woman who was interviewing for a job with a tech company called Skip The Dishes. Before the interview, she emailed the company and asked what the wages and benefits would look like for her position. The company, citing her interest in money over the company, rescinded their offer of an interview. The comments about this were split between people arguing that her question was inappropriate and people saying she was completely within her rights to ask. Some said employees have a right to know how much they're going to be paid for labor so they can decide if it's worth it to spend the money (on clothes, taking time off existing work, getting a babysitter, transit, and lots more) to come interview.

Other people argued it was impolite or "not proper etiquette" to ask about compensation before a job interview. Instead, you have to go in and make it seem like you're obsessed with the company and would work there for free, creating an illusion that people don't work for money. Fuck. That. Are we such kowtowing sniveling cowards that we have to let companies treat us like shit and pay us shit just to get a job—any job?

We reach dangerous territory when we deny ourselves

humanity just so we can land a job at a place that clearly expects us not to value pay, meaning they're going to pay next
to nothing for long hours and hard work.

You love people. You don't love companies (as the writer
Ashley C. Ford would say). Too many employers preach a
"family" atmosphere, but this is a manipulation tactic to stop
you from, out of guilt, asking for a promotion or higher salary or better conditions. Maybe they don't provide basic
health benefits; maybe they keep you overtime without compensation.

Not wanting to participate is not entitlement. When you
start willy-nilly labeling things "entitlement," you're on a
slippery slope to abetting the system and losing empathy.
And when you label that stuff that used to be basic as "entitlement," then you're allowing yourself to be treated poorly.
Is being able to buy food "entitlement"? Is having a place
to sleep "entitlement"? Is seeing a doctor when you're sick
"entitlement"? Aren't we all entitled to these things? Why
do we need to EARN our humanity in a country founded on
the idea that we have an inalienable right to life, liberty, and
the pursuit of happiness? By shrugging off these requests
as "entitlement," you're suggesting we don't have a right to
life-sustaining resources. And anyone who asks for more is
punished (or weeded out of the system by being unhirable or
fired).

Knowing my political stance, one of my Twitter followers tweeted me an Airbnb ad that said "renting out a room
in their house paid for their wedding." And I retweeted it
with the cheeky caption, "normalization." The replies to the
ad were brutal. "Sell your privacy off so you can afford a ba-

sic human rite of passage!" Instead of congratulating these people on allowing strangers to shit in their bathroom so they can ingeniously bring in enough extra income to marry, maybe ask why their day jobs don't afford them enough of a salary to do so or why wedding costs are jacked up so damn much. (Because they can price-gouge you for the fairy tale we're being sold, baby. It's all here in this book!)

———

In a *Jacobin* article, "Isn't America Already Kind of Socialist?" Chris Maisano cites a "widely noted [Princeton University] 2014 study by two political scientists that says the political dominance of the wealthy is so pronounced that average citizens exercise 'near zero' influence over government policymaking." (Thanks to Citizens United for the loosened campaign finance regulations.) What kind of power can we even have? #Resist, right? But I feel so overwhelmed and helpless.

Here comes my Charlie-Pepe Silvia moment: In 2008, the housing crisis hit. People our age started to realize shit was fucked up. So quickly, the baby boomer/media narrative became that millennials are "entitled." Getting involved in activism and socialism is "naive." Anyone who didn't agree with the status quo was mocked. Activism trails off. Around the 2016 election, it picks up again. More young people think: "Fuck, we gotta do something." Again, they're mocked, but this time they flock to the DSA in droves. They've realized that the easiest way to keep capitalism going is to paint movements against it as ridiculous social justice snowflake nonsense. Young people are on to this trick and are pushing back against it now. Peyton-Carrillo agreed. Those in power often tell him, "You don't know how this works," just so they can maintain power. (Think of the way the Right paints the Parkland shooting activists, for example.)

Some people don't revolt not because they don't care but because they have more pressing needs. When your life is consumed with needing to feed a family and/or yourself, with needing to pay off crushing medical debt, with needing to keep a roof over your head, or with any other daily issue, going on strike doesn't seem like a doable, affordable option. With the DSA in particular, it's a privilege to have the time to join and a privilege to have the education to even know what the organization is or does. Peyton-Carrillo said the DSA could work harder to reach out to marginalized communities, as the membership is predominantly white (a critique that often keeps people of color, like Peyton-Carrillo himself, from joining). When you're already marginalized, the hope needed to get involved in a movement like socialism can be lacking.

When I first started learning about capitalism, I lost it. *Why isn't everyone taking to the streets?!* I wondered. *We should all be furious!!!* But of course, people had taken to the streets— mostly young, white, middle-class people who could afford to camp out in Zuccotti Park during Occupy Wall Street. (According to *Fast Company*, 64 percent of protesters there in 2011 were younger than 34 years old, and the sample size of nonwhite participants was too small to even measure.)

Radical movements of all kinds tend to get co-opted by terrible white men. One prime example is the "Bernie Bros," Senator Bernie Sanders diehards who flooded my Instagram account during the 2016 election cycle with threats because

I wore a Hillary Clinton shirt in one photo (even after she'd been named the Democratic nominee). Fun!

Seth Masket of *Pacific Standard* magazine wrote an article, "The Whiteness of Bernie Sanders' Supporters," in 2016 that said that at that time, only 8 percent of African Americans were supporting Bernie (as opposed to 82 percent of African American voters supporting Clinton). Protecting marginalized people usually becomes protecting women, but always white women, and protecting the poor, but the white poor.

The most vulnerable—the people who could most benefit from the change Occupy—and later Bernie—promised, didn't have time to go to rallies. They had to work. Then the people who do have the time become the criticism du jour of the right-wingers, who point out that everyone working to dismantle the system is "privileged" and "idealistic" and "entitled" and "naive." Even I was skeptical of protesting during the time it would have benefited me most and when I had the most time to do it.

When I lived in New York in 2011, I went down to Zuccotti Park, where Occupy was happening, a couple times to check it out, but I wasn't looking to join this group of do-nothings. I still felt that incorrect, nagging voice telling me that financial strife was a personal intellectual and moral failing. I wouldn't be one of those people who blamed the system. I'd pull myself up by my bootstraps, the American way. I told myself I was different from these losers. If I joined these protesters, I'd be admitting defeat. I wanted to believe I was better. (After much research and a successful money podcast, I can now conclude I am not. None of us are.)

But my 2011 thoughts and doubts are how the system wins over and over again. (As Charlie from *It's Always Sunny* screamed, "THERE IS NO CAROL IN HR!!!!")

I'm still on the fence about the DSA, especially the holier-than-thou attitude I've seen displayed on social media, but it was nowhere to be heard in my delightful and engaging conversation with Peyton-Carrillo. I also completely understand the strong message and uncompromising opinions of the DSA as a result of the 2016 election. Going hard with open eyes and ears is not a bad option.

"It's time to quit losing, it's time to build something of your own, and this is the way forward to doing that. That's the pitch if I ever had to encounter somebody who was like, 'Well, I don't have time for it.' Things that are important for you and important for your survival, you make time for," Peyton-Carrillo said.

I think many people don't have the luxury to fight the status quo, but he replied, "I think the majority of people don't have the luxury to live in the status quo."

You've made it this far into the book. You know by now that marginalized people have been punished financially throughout history—women, people of color, LGBTQ people, disabled people, lower-class people, and those who are all of the above. There's the wage gap (which is much worse for women of color and trans women and those who are both), the lack of parental leave (which is much worse for women of color), the inability of women to get a credit card until the 1970s and even then, only with their husband's signature. (Everything is horrible!)

There are many, many deeply systemic hurdles to evening the playing field. In the illuminating 2015 book *2 Dollars a Day: Living on Almost Nothing in America*, researchers Kathryn Edin and H. Luke Schaefer profiled families who, forced off government assistance and unable to find jobs, had no other choice to but to live on that tiny titular amount a day. The two researchers found that in 2011, more than 4 percent of children in America were living on the same amount of money a middle-class person might spend at a toll booth. Schaefer's research counted family income, other cash income in the form of gifts from family and friends, odd jobs, private pensions, and any random money the family made. "The results of Schaefer's analysis were staggering," they wrote in their book. One and a half million families—almost 3 million children—were living on that metric of $2 a day per person.

A June 2017 article in the *Denver Post* revealed that "nowhere in America can a full-time minimum wage worker afford to rent a two-bedroom apartment." *Nowhere.* Even downsizing to a one-bedroom, Tracy Jan wrote in the *Post* piece, will only get you so far on minimum wage. Many people, even those getting welfare checks while working, still can't make enough to survive. The *Denver Post* article predicted, "Many of the occupations projected to add the most jobs by 2024 pay too little to cover rent."

When I first read it, I was surprised by this sweeping information, but Edin and Schaefer wouldn't be. In fact, they wrote, the number of people living on this amount of money doubled by 2011. "Although the rate of growth was high-

est among African Americans and Hispanics, nearly half the
2-dollar-a-day poor were white," Edin and Schaefer found.

So what are these families to do? Not only are they battling increasingly terrible living conditions, but they also
face horrible negative stereotypes about being lazy or conniving. "These moms don't play by the rules. These moms
don't control their fertility and they keep having children
that they can't afford. These moms are just sitting at home
collecting the checks," said Northwestern Sociology and African American Studies professor Celeste Watkins-Hayes as
examples of some of the preposterous reasons people give for
not liking government assistance or the people who need it.
"[It's] a sexy political tool to get people that are just above
welfare, people who are working class, or even people who
are middle class to say, 'Oh the reason why I'm economically
struggling isn't because of what the powerful are doing, it's
because of these women who can't get their act together,'"
Watkins-Hayes said.

Since when do our taxes have a morality clause? "We
shouldn't pay for other people's health care if we're healthy"
and "We shouldn't have to pay for irresponsible people" or
"Health care isn't a right, it's a commodity." My counterpoint
to the person saying these things is this: "I hope you'd say the
same thing if you ever lost everything."

———

In *2 Dollars a Day*, Edin wrote, "One way the poor pay for
government aid is with their time." In an eye-opening section of the book, she follows a woman named Modonna and

her daughter, residents of a homeless shelter who often go hungry on the weekends. Edin joined her as she waited in a line around the block to get into the Department of Human Services offices. First: You wait in that line. Then: You get a number. Wait. Get called in to see a caseworker. Provide the proper documents. Wait for your application to be approved. Wait for your Electronic Benefit Transfer (EBT) card and other assistance to come in the mail.

Modonna is turned down because she didn't arrive early enough and is berated by a worker there for doing so. She's told to come back tomorrow, which is something these applicants don't have the time or resources to do. Modonna gave up that day, defeated. In Watkins-Hayes's research, the main reason people don't get welfare or stop receiving welfare is because of the "administrative hassle."

"These meetings, the paperwork, the scrutiny, the surveillance, it's just like, enough of this," Watkins-Hayes said. It's that way on purpose. "According to politicians, it's not supposed to be a fun and easy process, because they want to discourage usage. So they want all that paperwork, and they want it to be time consuming and they want it to feel like you're being highly scrutinized."

I'm a weenie. I won't go back to a grocery store if I've had an awkward encounter with a cashier, so the humiliation and frustration of Modonna's experience is horrible. A page later in the book, Edin and Schaefer quote another woman, Susan Brown, who says, "I just don't want to get rejected again." They wrote that she cries "uncontrollably" every time she gets turned down by a potential employer or government agency. Her heart can't take much more rejection. I don't blame her.

TAKEAWAYS

- The structures we have collectively created and live in are not working for the vast majority of us, but we can also collectively build a different system.
- If we're all so "bad with money," maybe the problem isn't us. Maybe it's the confusing and inaccessible ways how money and power are organized. Maybe it's the dark history integral to our country's financial system. Probably it's both.
- In the meantime, we need to try to understand the system, because most of us have to live in it. We can't dismantle it, work to fix what's broken, or engage politically if we can't even begin to understand it.

WE ARE ALL KURT RUSSELL

In director John Carpenter's 1982 horror film, *The Thing*, the crew of an isolated Antarctic research base, led by a never-hotter Kurt Russell, is attacked by a shapeshifting alien. The monster can look like anyone, so instead of working together to defeat it, the snow-trapped crew turns on each other. This is what the monster wants.

Money is the alien. We are all Kurt Russell.

Money is purposefully disorienting and confusing. Everyone's journey with it is personal. There's no such thing as advice everyone should take, and every piece of advice works differently for every person's lifestyle and circumstances. The only mistake you've made is maybe you believed this was an isolating problem that said something about your character and intelligence. It isn't, and it doesn't.

The reason I'm so dedicated to sharing all my money

ugliness is that we need to end the fallacy that we can't, or shouldn't, talk about money. I used to be absolutely terrified of frankly and openly discussing money. I took that fear, and I made thinking about and researching and speaking out about money into my full-time job. I know more than I did when I intentionally avoided anything financial, but—after hours and days and months and years of looking into every aspect of this stuff—I still don't know everything. Honestly, I barely know enough.

The system is a winding labyrinth of paperwork and jargon and debt and dead-ends. I'm much more aware, but I'm far from an expert.

You don't have to be an expert. Hardly anyone is. But you *do* have to pay attention. It sucks. It super sucks. I know it sucks. But unfortunately you can't opt out of dealing with money, and in the past few years, I've opened my eyes to my own financial reality, and as a result my financial *feelings*, if not my actual situation, *have* gotten better.

I made more money this past year than in any other year of my life, and it helped me that when that happened, I didn't panic. I didn't anxiously, compulsively spend it all. I paid down most of my debts: medical debt, credit card debt, auto loan, two of my three student loans. I started saving a little for retirement. I still have a constantly fluctuating amount in my savings account. I've still somehow acquired more credit card debt through my continued irresponsibility. I am far from perfect and still mess up ALL THE TIME.

But I let go of the total power money had over my psyche. Money isn't this huge, secret monster anymore. *Everyone* has intense emotions and unique problems connected to money.

We all have to face and think about and use money. Even if we moved to the woods, I assume there'd be some sort of bartering system we'd have to set up with the deer and the squirrels.

Our money scripts aren't carved into stone. I've worked hard to change mine. Where we start off can't be helped. What can be helped is how we feel about it and how we address it.

Once we do that, we can stop individualizing issues that are collective. There are deep systemic reasons that large swaths of people are all on uneven footing. Everyone who has the time and means, especially upper-middle-class millennials and Gen Z, needs to be on top of legislation, elections, and economic and financial news. The larger system and those in power want us to internalize shame and fear around money, beat ourselves up, and believe the propaganda that the rich deserve their wealth and the poor deserve to struggle instead of looking outward at the fucked-up status quo.

It's hard to spend an entire book both giving advice and telling you the cards are stacked against you. After all that, it's even harder to say the solution is to rise up, join hands, and suddenly inject everyone on the planet with some much-needed empathy. There should be a middle ground. One where personal responsibility takes into account all the systemic factors. Where we don't shame low-income people for "moral failings" that are due in large part to histories of oppression and classist legislation. (And for God's sake, let them buy whatever they want.)

We can pay off our student loans while knowing that taking them out in the first place may not be the best path for our children and while advocating politically for forgiveness programs. We can save for retirement while also knowing that starving ourselves of life's little pleasures or working ourselves to exhaustion isn't the only road. We can prepare for future medical debts while still calling our congressional representatives or running for office ourselves to put universal health care in place.

Professor William Darity's findings on wealth inequality are too staggering to be one person's responsibility. "The key thing is, you cannot close these gaps through autonomous, individual action," he said. "These gaps will not be closed by the people who have little income behaving differently, making different decisions. The magnitudes of these gaps have nothing to do with the personal or individual decisions people make about their finances."

And so as I finish up a book telling you what to do about money problems, I have to take my own advice because my finances are still not good. They may never be as good as I want them to be. They'll go through phases of better and then worse and then better and then worse than ever before. Even though I made "money" into my full-time job, something I suspect not everyone has the time or inclination to do, I *still* don't have an infallible handle on my accounts. I still have so much to learn before I reach full financial competence, and even then I can't predict what will happen in my future.

There's racial, classist, ableist, transphobic, homophobic, and misogynist tints to money that can't be ignored. Black and Latinx trans women suffer a wider wage and employment gap than cis white women. People with disabilities on SSI can't save as much as they'd like to. Cancer survivors have medical debt that is considered "cosmetic" and not covered by insurance. There's no good person or bad person when it comes to money. As Clio Chang wrote in her piece about the "empathy gap," being part of a society doesn't mean resources are just for the people we like; it means resources are for everyone, even the people we actively don't like. This alien affects everyone. So while you work to better your own money situation, you also *have* to look at the big picture.

It's really hard to do both when it comes to money, but we can't be like that crew in Antarctica, guys. We can't let it tear us apart.

ACKNOWLEDGMENTS

First, I thank Nona Willis Aronowitz, the wonderful editor who kicked all this off with my viral "Get Rich or Die Vlogging" piece, made infinitely better by her notes. My research assistant, Emily Parsons, did a lot of grunt work with a smile. My *Bad with Money* producers Sam Dingman and Lindsey Kradowill are both saints; the podcast is theirs as much as it is mine. Further research was conducted by Paul Haynes and Jill Gutowitz, who transcribed and listened to my voice more than anyone would want to.

I thank my editors Daniella Wexler and Haley Weaver, and my team and cheerleaders Matt Sadeghian, Chloe Pisello, and Sasha Raskin.

I thank Jess Aceves and the students of Gage Park High School, Sallie Middleton and the students of Palm Beach State College, and Maggie Sherman and the students of Plantation High School. I watched Stevie Boebi's video on homeless youth and read posts by Talia Jane while writing this book, and they provided much needed perspective.

I thank Marc and Caryn Dunn for their patience and honesty. What a wild ride we've all been on. I love you both. I thank Cheyanne Dunn for her contributions to the book and my life. I'd be remiss if I didn't mention the queen herself: Meme, who taught me to be unapologetic and a necessary amount of selfish. Meme passed away during the editing of this book and I am thankful I got to interview her for it before then. Her story deserves to be told.

I thank Allison Raskin for always pushing me to be better. Suh dude.

I also thank my therapist, *The L Word*, and *Law and Order SVU* for their support during the writing of this book. Everyone else mentioned in a positive light in this book, thank you for your contributions. And thank you to the LGBTQ community for always caring about what I'm up to. I do pretty much everything to make you all proud.

BIBLIOGRAPHY

Andrews, Michelle. "Medical Debt Is Top Reason Consumers Hear from Collection Agencies." NPR, January 24, 2017. www.npr.org /sections/health-shots/2017/01/24/511269991/medical-debt -is-top-reason-consumers-hear-from-collection-agencies.

Apatow, Judd. *Sick in the Head: Conversations about Life and Comedy*. London: Duckworth Overlook, 2017.

Ashford, Kate. "More Parents Taking On Their Kids' College Debt." *Forbes*, December 29, 2016. www.forbes.com/sites/kateashford /2016/12/29/college-debt/#36c27ecf4a86.

Astone, Nan Marie, Steven Martin, and H. E. Elizabeth Peters. "Millennial Childbearing and the Recession." Washington, DC: Urban Institute, 2015. www.urban.org/sites/default/files/publication /49796/2000203-Millennial-Childbearing-and-the-Recession.pdf.

Avery, Dan. "Gay Couples Are Spending More on Weddings, Asking for Mom and Dad's Blessing, since Marriage Equality." *LOGO News*, June 28, 2016. www.newnownext.com/gay-couples-are

-spending-more-on-weddings-asking-for-mom-and-dads
-blessing-since-marriage-equality/06/2016/.

"Avoiding the Probate Process." *Findlaw,* n.d. estate.findlaw.com
/probate/avoiding-the-probate-process.html.

Backman, Maurie. "How Much Should the Average American Save
for Retirement?" *Motley Fool,* July 17, 2017. www.fool.com
/retirement/2017/07/17/how-much-should-the-average
-american-save-for-reti.aspx.

Beck, Jackie. "Debt and Suicide: Killing Yourself over Debt." September 10, 2016. https://www.jackiebeck.com/debt-and-suicide
-killing-yourself-over-debt/.

"Become a Surrogate: Surrogate Mothers Make Dreams Come True!"
ConceiveAbilities, n.d. www.conceiveabilities.com/surrogates
/become-a-surrogate-mother.

Berger, Sarah. "Side Hustle Nation: Millennials Are Making Major
Money with Side Gigs." *Bankrate,* January 5, 2018. www.bankrate
.com/personal-finance/smart-money/side-hustles-survey/.

blindspy. "It's Always Sunny in Philadelphia: Pepe Silvia." YouTube,
March 1, 2012. www.youtube.com/watch?v=_nTpsv9PNqo.

Bonner, Mehera. "Five Reasons You Should Definitely Skip Your
Wedding." *Marie Claire,* January 20, 2015. www.marieclaire.com
/sex-love/news/a13060/5-reasons-you-should-definitely-skip
-your-wedding/.

Brinkley-Badgett, Constance. "What Does FICO Stand For?"
Credit.com, April, 2018, https://www.credit.com/credit-scores
/what-does-fico-stand-for-and-what-is-a-fico-credit-score/.

Bursch, Dan. "What Every Intern Gets Wrong about Landing a
Job." *Fortune,* July 19, 2016, fortune.com/2016/07/18/internship
-full-time-job-search/.

Byrnes, Taylor. "Applied for a Job at @SkipTheDishes. They Cancelled My Interview b/c I Asked about Wages/Benefits."
Twitter, March 12, 2017. twitter.com/feministjourney/status

/841156011780116480/photo/1?tfw_creator=http%3A%2F
%2Ftwitter.com%2FiD4RO&tfw_site=BuzzFeedCanada
&ref_src=twsrc%5Etfw&ref_url=https%3A%2F%2Fwww
.buzzfeed.com%2Fishmaeldaro%2Fskip-the-wages.

Caldwell, Miriam. "Budgeting and Personal Finance." *Balance*, April 2018. www.thebalance.com/budgeting-4074043.

Calfas, Jennifer. "Millennials Have Very Different Values Than Older Americans." *Time*, April 20, 2017. time.com/4748357/millennials -values-census-report/.

Captain, Sean. "The Demographics of Occupy Wall Street." *Fast Company*, October 19, 2011. www.fastcompany.com/1789018 /demographics-occupy-wall-street.

Carpenter, John, director. *The Thing*. 1982.

CBSNewsOnline. "Author: Suze Orman's Advice Won't Save Your Finances." YouTube, January 23, 2013. www.youtube.com /watch?v=b-Ad4JIfao4.

Chang, Clio. "Ending the Empathy Gap." *Jacobin*, March 21, 2017. www.jacobinmag.com/2017/03/frank-rich-response-new-york -magazine-trump-ryan-chaffetz-obamacare.

"Check Out the Latte Factor, and Get Started Today!" N.d. davidbach.com/latte-factor/.

Chesler, Caren. "How Parents Solve Their Kids' Big Debt Crisis." *Fiscal Times*, December 21, 2011. www.thefiscaltimes.com/Articles /2011/12/21/How-Parents-Solve-Their-Kids-Big-Debt-Crisis.

"Comparing the Costs of Domestic, International and Foster Care Adoption." *American Adoptions*. N.d. www.americanadoptions .com/adopt/the_costs_of_adopting.

Cruze, Rachel. "A Quick Guide to Your Emergency Fund." DaveRamsey.com.https://www.daveramsey.com/blog/quick -guide-to-your-emergency-fund.

"Debt Buyers: Last Week Tonight with John Oliver (HBO)." YouTube, June 5, 2016. www.youtube.com/watch?v=hxUAntt1z2c.

Dentata, Amy. "I Am Literally Not Allowed to Have More than $2,000 in My Bank Account Due to Disability." Twitter, November 1, 2017. twitter.com/AmyDentata/status/925758973126443008.

DePersio, Greg. "How Much Money Do You Need to Live in Los Angeles?" *Investopedia*, September 14, 2017. www.investopedia .com/articles/personal-finance/091415/how-much-money-do -you-need-live-los-angeles.asp.

DeSilver, Drew. "Five Facts about Social Security." Pew Research Center, August 18, 2015. www.pewresearch.org/fact-tank/2015 /08/18/5-facts-about-social-security/.

Dilworth, Kelly. "Average Card APR Remains at Record High of 16.32 Percent." CreditCards.com, January 10, 2018. https://www .creditcards.com/credit-card-news/interest-rate-report-011018 -unchanged-2121.php/.

"Disputing Errors on Credit Reports." *Consumer Information*, February 2017. www.consumer.ftc.gov/articles/0151-disputing-errors -credit-reports.

"Donations and Tax Deductions." GoFundMe Help Center, n.d. support.gofundme.com/hc/en-us/articles/203604684-Donations -and-Tax-Deductions.

Donnelly, Grace. "Unpacking the Study That Claims 1 in 6 Millennials Has $100K Saved." *Fortune*, January 24, 2018. fortune.com /2018/01/24/millennials-saving-money/.

"Donor Insemination." American Pregnancy Association, September 2, 2016, americanpregnancy.org/infertility/donor-insemination/.

Dunn, Gaby. "Get Rich or Die Vlogging: The Sad Economics of Internet Fame." *Splinter*, December 14, 2015. splinternews.com /get-rich-or-die-vlogging-the-sad-economics-of-internet -1793853578.

Edin, Kathryn J., and H. Luke. Shaefer. *$2.00 a Day: Living on Almost Nothing in America*. New York: Houghton Mifflin Harcourt, 2015.

Egg Donation." Center for Human Reproduction, www.centerfor humanreprod.com/egg-donation/how-it-works/.

"Dr. Jill Biden Wants to Make Community College Free." *Late Night with Seth Meyers.* YouTube, November 5, 2015. www.youtube.com/watch?v=aMh4rpgw7bM.

Elkins, Kathleen. "After Living on $60 a Week for a Month, Here Are My 7 Best Money-Saving Tips." CNBC, January 27, 2017. www.cnbc.com/2017/01/27/after-a-month-on-a-cash-diet-here-are-my-best-money-saving-tips.html.

"Emerson College." In *The Princeton Review College Rankings and Reviews.* N.d. princetonreview.com/college/emerson-college-1022990.

Erb, Kelly Phillips. "Ask TheTaxgirl: Deducting the Cost of Birth Control." *Forbes,* March 13, 2013. www.forbes.com/sites/kellyphillipserb/2013/03/13/ask-the-taxgirl-deducting-the-cost-of-birth-control/#d293adc1291e.

Fleshler, David. "Alligator Hunters May Be Able to Use Handguns." *Sun Sentinel,* November 26, 2012. articles.sun-sentinel.com/2012-11-26/news/fl-gator-rules-20121123_1_alligator-population-alligator-hunters-harry-dutton.

"For Egg Donors." Center for Human Reproduction, n.d. www.centerforhumanreprod.com/egg-donation/donors/faqs.

Franck, Thomas. "Nearly Half of Millennials Haven't Starting Saving for Retirement: Wells Fargo." *CNBC,* August 30, 2017. www.cnbc.com/2017/08/30/nearly-half-of-millennials-havent-starting-saving-for-retirement-wells-fargo.html.

Freeman, Andrea. "Racism in the Credit Card Industry." *North Carolina Law Review* 95 (2017), 1073–1145. scholarship.law.unc.edu/cgi/viewcontent.cgi?article=4957&context=nclr.

Gabler, Neal. "The Secret Shame of Middle-Class Americans." *Atlantic,* April 26, 2016. www.theatlantic.com/magazine/archive/2016/05/my-secret-shame/476415/.

"Gen Z Research—2017 National Study on Generation Z – GEN HQ." GEN HQ, n.d. genhq.com/gen-z-2017/.

Gerson Uffalussy, Jennifer. "The Cost of IVF: 4 Things I Learned While Battling Infertility." *Forbes,* February 6, 2014. www.forbes

.com/sites/learnvest/2014/02/06/the-cost-of-ivf-4-things-i
-learned-while-battling-infertility/#29493e2024dd.

Gillespie, Patrick. "Intuit: Gig Economy Is 34% of US Workforce."
CNNMoney, May 24, 2017. money.cnn.com/2017/05/24/news
/economy/gig-economy-intuit/index.html.

Glum, Julia. "Generation Z Teens Play It Conservative." *Newsweek*,
May 7, 2017. http://www.newsweek.com/generation-z-saving
-money-retirement-not-millennials-595679.

Golden, Paul. "Nearly 60 Percent of Parents Financially Supporting Adult Children." National Endowment for Financial Education, May 26, 2011. www.nefe.org/Press-Room/News/Parents-
Financially-Supporting-Adult-Children.

Greenhouse, Steven. "The Unpaid Intern, Legal or Not." *New York
Times*, April 3, 2010. www.nytimes.com/2010/04/03/business
/03intern.html?pagewanted=all.

Hagaman, Austin. "Major Differences between Retirement Plans—
401k vs. IRA vs. Roth IRA." Withum Wealth, Private Wealth
Management, May 15, 2012. www.pwm-nj.com/knowledge/tax
/401k-ira-roth-ira.

Holkar, Merlyn, and Polly MacKenzie. "Money and Mental Health
Facts and Statistics." Money and Mental Health Policy Institute,
June 13, 2016. www.moneyandmentalhealth.org/money-and
-mental-health-facts/.

"How Does Gage Park High School Rank Among America's Best
High Schools?" *U.S. News & World Report*, 2018. www.usnews.com
/education/best-high-schools/illinois/districts/chicago-public
-schools/gage-park-high-school-6559.

"How Much Do Surrogates Get Paid? A Look at Surrogate Compensation." *Southern Surrogacy*, n.d. southernsurrogacy.com/surrogates
/financial-benefits/.

"How Much Does a Groom's Suit or Tuxedo Cost?" *CostHelper*, n.d.
weddings.costhelper.com/groom-tuxedo.html.

"How We Screen Sperm Donors." Seattle Sperm Bank, January 27, 2017. www.seattlespermbank.com/how-we-screen-sperm-donors/.

Howe, Neil. "The Unhappy Rise of the Millennial Intern." *Forbes*, April 22, 2014. https://www.forbes.com/sites/realspin/2014/04/22/the-unhappy-rise-of-the-millennial-intern/#31709de71328.

Inheriting Debt from a Family Member. Commonwealth Financial Network, 2014. www.commonwealth.com/RepSiteContent/inheriting-debt.htm.

Irby, Latoya. "Five Reasons Why Good Credit Matters." *Balance*, March 18, 2018. https://www.thebalance.com/reasons-why-good-credit-matters-960178.

"Is a Credit Union Right for Me?" MyCreditUnion.Gov. n.d. www.mycreditunion.gov/about-credit-unions/Pages/Is-a-Credit-Union-Right-for-Me.aspx.

"Is It Possible to Not Have a Credit Report?" *Experian*, July 16, 2016. https://www.experian.com/blogs/ask-experian/it-is-possible-to-not-have-a-credit-report//.

"Is the Affordable Care Act Working?" *New York Times*, October 27, 2014. https://www.nytimes.com/interactive/2014/10/27/us/is-the-affordable-care-act-working.html.

Jacobs, Sarah. "The Average Wedding Cost in America Is Over $30,000." *BusinessInsider*, April 2, 2018. http://www.businessinsider.com/average-wedding-cost-in-america-most-expensive-2018-3.

Jacobson, Ivy. "Thirteen Legal Benefits of Marriage." Theknot.com, n.d. www.theknot.com/content/benefits-of-marriage.

Jan, Tracy. "Nowhere in America Can a Full-Time Minimum Wage Worker Afford to Rent a Two-Bedroom Apartment." *Denver Post*, June 12, 2017. www.denverpost.com/2017/06/09/minimum-wage-rent-two-bedroom-apartment/?preview_id=2678080.

Kagel, Tamara Shayne. "Why You Shouldn't Sign a Prenup." *Huffington Post*, January 12, 2015. www.huffingtonpost.com/tamara-shayne-kagel/why-you-shouldnt-sign-a-prenup_b_6141470.html.

Kaiser, Bilal. "What Is Probate?" *Legalzoom.com*, January 2009. www .legalzoom.com/articles/what-is-probate.

Kenney, Caitlin. "Why Do Wedding Dresses Cost So Much?" *Slate*, YouTube, April 9, 2012. www.youtube.com/watch?v =b7SY53OuD3U.

Kowarski, Ilana. "Fifty Colleges with the Highest Application Fees." *U.S. News & World Report*, October 10, 2017. www.usnews.com /education/best-colleges/the-short-list-college/articles/2017 -10-10/50-colleges-with-the-highest-application-fees.

"LGBTQ Activist Cleve Jones: 'I'm Well Aware How Fragile Life Is.'" NPR, November 29, 2016. www.npr.org/templates/transcript /transcript.php?storyId=503724044.

"Loan Consolidation." Federal Student Aid, September 12, 2017. studentaid.ed.gov/sa/repay-loans/consolidation.

Maisano, Chris. "Isn't America Already Kind of Socialist?" *Jacobin*, January 27, 2016. www.jacobinmag.com/2016/01/democratic -socialism-government-bernie-sanders-primary-president.

Marquand, Barbara. "How Much Life Insurance Do I Need?" Nerd-Wallet, July 28, 2017. www.nerdwallet.com/blog/insurance/how -much-life-insurance-do-i-need/.

Martin, Emmie. "Here's How Much More Expensive It Is for You to Go to College Than It Was for Your Parents." *CNBC*, November 29, 2017. www.cnbc.com/2017/11/29/how-much-college -tuition-has-increased-from-1988-to-2018.html.

Martin, Manjula. "Who Pays Writers?" n.d. whopayswriters.com /#/results.

Masket, Seth. "The Whiteness of Bernie Sanders' Supporters." *Pacific Standard*, February 15, 2016. psmag.com/news/the-whiteness -of-bernie-sanders-supporters.

Mulhere, Kaitlin. "This High School Senior Is Spending $1,700 on College Applications. Is That Insane or Normal?" *Time*, December 26, 2017. http://time.com/money/5072196/college -application-fees-high-school-seniors/.

————. "Credit Scores: This Is the Average for Every Age Group." *Time*, January 23, 2018. time.com/money/5112478 /average-credit-score-by-age/.

NACE Staff. "Paid Interns/Co-Ops See Greater Offer Rates and Salary Offers Than Their Unpaid Classmates." March 23, 2016. www.naceweb.org/job-market/internships/paid-interns-co-ops -see-greater-offer-rates-and-salary-offers-than-their-unpaid -classmates/.

"New Citi/Seventeen Survey: College Students Take Control of Their Financial Futures." *Business Wire*, August 7, 2013. www .businesswire.com/news/home/20130807005644/en/New -CitiSeventeen-Survey-College-Students-Control-Financial.

Newport, Frank. "Americans' Views of Socialism, Capitalism Are Little Changed." Gallup.com, May 6, 2016. news.gallup.com /poll/191354/americans-views-socialism-capitalism-little -changed.aspx.

Nichols, James Michael. "Here's Why 'What Outfit Do You Want to Be Buried In?' Is Something You Should Think About." *Huffington Post*, February 2, 2016. www.huffingtonpost.com/2015/03/17 /vamonos-queer-film_n_6886390.html.

Nir, Sarah Maslin. "The Price of Nice Nails." *New York Times*, May 7, 2015. www.nytimes.com/2015/05/10/nyregion/at-nail-salons -in-nyc-manicurists-are-underpaid-and-unprotected.html ?mtrref=www.google.com&gwh=821A9ACC3DE6C12BD 5155AF3EDBCB3D0&gwt=pay.

Olen, Helaine. *Pound Foolish: Exposing the Dark Side of the Personal Finance Industry*. New York: Portfolio/Penguin, 2012.

O'Shea, Arielle. "What Millennials Get Wrong about Retirement." NerdWallet, June 22, 2016. www.nerdwallet.com/blog/investing /what-millennials-get-wrong-retirement/.

Pant, Paula. "How to Manage Your Budget Using the 50/30/20 Budgeting Rule." *Balance*, February 4, 2018. www.thebalance .com/the-50-30-20-rule-of-thumb-453922.

———. "Try This Simple 5-Category Budget to Help You Manage Your Money." *Balance*, April 30, 2018. www.thebalance.com/try-the-simple-5-category-budget-453622.

Penty, Rob. "What I Learned about Money after My Parents Died." *Billfold*, November 3, 2015. www.thebillfold.com/2015/11/what-i-learned-about-money-after-my-parents-died/.

Perhach, Paulette. "A Story of a Fuck Off Fund." *Billfold*, August 15. 2017. www.thebillfold.com/2016/01/a-story-of-a-fuck-off-fund/.

Petersen, Anne Helen. "The Real Problem with Crowdfunding Health Care." BuzzFeed, March 11, 2017. www.buzzfeed.com/annehelenpetersen/real-peril-of-crowdfunding-healthcare?utm_term=.yyBKlnGmd#.qeYwLY7N0.

Popper, Nathaniel. "What Is Bitcoin, and How Does It Work?" *New York Times*, October 1, 2017. www.nytimes.com/2017/10/01/technology/what-is-bitcoin-price.html.

Postal, Leslie. "Florida Ranks 29th in Nation on Education Quality on Annual Report Card." OrlandoSentinel.com, January 4, 2017. www.orlandosentinel.com/features/education/os-florida-education-quality-annual-report-20170104-story.html.

"Power of Attorney." Wikimedia Foundation, April 29, 2018. en.wikipedia.org/wiki/Power_of_attorney.

"Predatory Lending: Last Week Tonight with John Oliver." Performance by John Oliver, YouTube, HBO, August 10, 2014. www.youtube.com/watch?v=PDylgzybWAw.

Ragusa, Gina. "Research Shows How Generation Z Thinks Differently from Millennials When It Comes to Money." *Business Insider*, June 7, 2017. www.businessinsider.com/differences-between-generation-z-and-millennials-money-2017-6?r=UK&IR=T.

Redmond, Ashley. "Here's What Social Security Will Look Like by the Time Millennials Retire." *Huffington Post*, December 6, 2017. www.huffingtonpost.com/gobankingrates/heres-what-social-securit_b_8023246.html.

"Repayment Plans." Federal Student Aid, March 8, 2018. studentaid
.ed.gov/sa/repay-loans/understand/plans.

Rivas, Jorge. "When It Comes to Maternity Leave, Latinas May Have
It the Worst." Splinternews.com, May 11, 2015. splinternews
.com/when-it-comes-to-maternity-leave-latinas-may-have-it
-t-1793847687.

Rubenstein, Edwin. "How Millennials Are Slowing U.S. Population
Growth and Enhancing Sustainability." Negative Population
Growth, November 2017. www.npg.org/wp-content/uploads
/2017/11/MillennialsEnhancingSustainability-FP-2017.pdf.

"A Same-Sex Couple's Guide to Wedding Planning." TheNotAdam,
YouTube, May 19, 2016. www.youtube.com/watch?v=I42p62G
xkDo.

Sanger-Katz, Margot. "Grading Obamacare: Successes, Failures and
'Incompletes'." New York Times, February 5, 2017. www.nytimes
.com/2017/02/05/upshot/grading-obamacare-successes-failures
-and-incompletes.html?mtrref=www.google.com.

Seaver, Maggie. "The National Average Cost of a Wedding Hits
$35,329." Theknot.com, 2016. www.theknot.com/content/average
-wedding-cost-2016.

Searle, Sarah Winifred. "'You'll Be Just Fine': A Comic by Sarah Winifred Searle." Rewire.News, February 2, 2017. rewire.news/article
/2017/02/02/youll-just-fine-comic-sarah-winifred-searle/.

Servon, Lisa J. The Unbanking of America: How the New Middle Class
Survives. Boston: Mariner Books, 2018.

Shaw, Alexis. "Dr. Jill Biden Explains Why Community College Is
'One of America's Best-Kept Secrets.'" AOL.com, July 15, 2016.
www.aol.com/article/2015/11/05/dr-jill-biden-explains-why
-community-college-is-one/21259058/.

Sheffield, Hazel. "Your Mental Health Is Making You Poor." Vice,
August 11, 2016. www.vice.com/sv/article/4w5vp9/why-your
-mental-health-is-making-you-poor.

Sherman, Rachel. "What the Rich Won't Tell You." *New York Times*, September 8, 2017. www.nytimes.com/2017/09/08/opinion/sunday /what-the-rich-wont-tell-you.html.

Siegel, Lee. "Why I Defaulted on My Student Loans." *New York Times*, June 6, 2015. www.nytimes.com/2015/06/07/opinion/sunday /why-i-defaulted-on-my-student-loans.html?_r=0.

Silver, Nate. "Why Young Democrats Love Bernie Sanders." FiveThirtyEight, February 8, 2016. fivethirtyeight.com/features /why-young-democrats-love-bernie-sanders/.

Smith, Aaron. "Gig Work, Online Selling and Home Sharing." Pew Research Center: Internet, Science & Tech, November 17, 2016. www.pewinternet.org/2016/11/17/gig-work-online-selling -and-home-sharing/.

———. "Why Join the Gig Economy? For Many, the Answer Is 'for Fun.'" Pew Research Center, November 18, 2016. www.pewresearch .org/fact-tank/2016/11/18/why-join-the-gig-economy-for-many -the-answer-is-for-fun/.

Smith, Michelle. "Ten Best Retirement Plan Options." *Motley Fool*, November 18, 2015. www.fool.com/investing/general/2015/11 /18/10-best-retirement-plan-options.aspx.

"Social Security." *Social Security History*, n.d. www.ssa.gov/planners /retire/divspouse.html.

Stein, Jeff. "Nine Questions about the Democratic Socialists of America You Were Too Embarrassed to Ask." *Vox*, August 5, 2017. www.vox.com/policy-and-politics/2017/8/5/15930786/dsa -socialists-convention-national.

Stein, Joel. "Millennials: The Me Me Me Generation." *Time*, May 20, 2013. time.com/247/millennials-the-me-me-me-generation/.

Stempel, Jonathan. "Viacom to Pay $7.21 Million to End Interns Wage Lawsuit." *Huffington Post*, May 13, 2015. www.huffingtonpost .com/2015/03/13/viacom-settlement-intern-wage-lawsuit _n_6854808.html.

"Stigma Definition in the Cambridge English Dictionary." *Cambridge Dictionary*. dictionary.cambridge.org/us/dictionary/english/stigma.

Strauss, Karsten. "Do Millennials Think Differently about Money and Career?" *Forbes*, September 18, 2013. www.forbes.com/sites /karstenstrauss/2013/09/17/do-millennials-think-differently -about-money-and-career/.

"Take Action for Reproductive Justice: Fund Abortions!" DC Abortion Fund, November 27, 2016. dcabortionfund.org/2016/11 /take-action-for-reproductive-justice-fund-abortions/.

Taylor, Chris. "When Bipolar Disorder Leads to Extreme Shopping." Reuters, June 19, 2013. www.reuters.com/article/spending-bipolar /your-money-when-bipolar-disorder-leads-to-extreme-shopping -idUSL2N0EP1A220130619.

"Tiffany Haddish Played 'White Phoebe' in Jay-Z's 'Friends' Parody." YouTube, August 16, 2017, www.youtube.com/watch?v=ilotZq zaZgU.

"Top Five Reasons That Men Choose to Be Sperm Donors." Sperm Bank of California. donors.thespermbankofca.org/.

"2016 Fidelity Investments Millennial Money Study: Facts, Figures and Findings." 2016, www.fidelity.com/bin-public/060_www _fidelity_com/documents/pr/millennial-money-fact-sheet.pdf.

"2018 Wedding Report." *WeddingWire*, go.weddingwire.com/newly wed-report.

"Types of Retirement Plans." US Department of Labor, May 6, 2016. www.dol.gov/general/topic/retirement/typesofplans.

Tyson, Eric. *Personal Finance for Dummies*. Hoboken, NJ: Wiley, 2016.

Ward, Marguerite. "The 10 Companies with the Best Summer Internships, According to Current Interns." *CNBC*, August 24, 2017. www.cnbc.com/2017/08/09/the-10-companies-with-the-best -summer-internships-according-to-current-interns.html.

"The Wedding Report." Weddings, 2006. www.bridalassociation ofamerica.com/Wedding_Statistics/.

Weiss, Rob. "More Students Expected to Help Pay for College as Parents Become Less Worried about Costs." Press release, Discover Financial Services, 2016. investorrelations.discover.com/newsroom /press-releases/press-release-details/2016/More-Students -Expected-to-Help-Pay-for-College-as-Parents-Become-Less -Worried-about-Costs/default.aspx.

Wexler, Ellen. "Paying to Work." *Inside Higher Ed*, May 17, 2016. www.insidehighered.com/news/2016/05/17/when-students -pay-tuition-work-unpaid-internships.

"Why Are Weddings so Damn Expensive?" *Vox*, July 30, 2015, www .youtube.com/watch?time_continue=272&v=YxEa_SpL_Fs.

"Will Social Security Still Exist When I Retire?" *Time*, n.d. time.com /money/collection-post/2791251/will-social-security-still -exist-when-i-retire/.

Wohner, Robert. "5 Things I Learned From Participating in Clinical Trials." *Thought Catalog*, April 20, 2012. thoughtcatalog .com/robert-wohner/2012/04/5-things-i-learned-from -participating-in-clinical-trials/.

INDEX